Good Bob Bad Bob

Two Paths to Success in Sales

By: Bob Bloom

Dedicated to: Big Al
Loved you, Pops

Table of Contents

It is Simple. It is Not Easy.

I am neither cool, nor am I pretending to be. I am just a guy who loves to share. If you ask enough questions, you yearn to share, what you have learned. That is what I hope to do, with you.

Please be lenient in your judgment of my work. I am old, kinda, sorta chronologically. I do not profess to be anybody but B-O-B. Let each chapter stand-alone. If you don't have an "Aha" with one, read on. I cover many concepts that I love.

This book is a collection of a few of my thoughts and some thoughts, of others. Things have blended together so much, that the lines of distinction, are foggy. I will do my best to interpret what I have learned from others, but won't be able to resist adding my own spin....

I believe that achieving success is simple. It is not easy.
(that is a sample of my spin adding)

As you open Chapter One, open your mind to a new look at things. Stop and ask yourself, how you stack up, in each chapter. Take the data and you decide.

Over the last few years, I have interviewed a lot of you, who are better than me. I thank those, who so openly shared with me their, thoughts and models. You know who you are. Thank you.

I hope that you, readers, succeed and pass on your knowledge to another. You are supposed to receive and then you are supposed to give.

It is simple. It is not easy.

The Vote is in

The "Eyes" have it

1st Question to Ask a Prospect

We are all aware of the importance of the infamous, "First Impression." How important it is, to immediately leave a favorable impression, with our potential client, or our fate may be sealed, before we open our mouth.

To add extra pressure to that moment, I would like to add, that the success of your entire relationship with this person, could actually revolve around their answer to your initial question. The subtleties of their answering process, tell it all.

Tell it all that is, if you ask the right question. Ask the wrong question and the opportunity is lost. The art of "Question #1," separates the winners from the losers. Start with something like, "Nice to meet you sir. How are you?"… and as the chant goes…. It's all over….

The first question, is vitally important. I suggest you go with something like: "When you were a kid, what color, was your favorite lunchbox?" A classic. Or  perhaps, your style leans towards: "What is your 3rd and 4th favorite, type of dog?" I love that one and it is quite effective, though I personally lean towards the lunchbox query. Steal my ideas and tweak my words. Make them your own. You might choose a different question to start the conversation with, but do not stray far. What do these two queries have in common? They are not easily answered, without taking a moment to remember back and recall. It requires the prospect, to think and not just answer, with something, that is on the tip of their tongue. Ask their favorite color and they respond blue, without thinking. Asking their 3rd favorite color, requires thought, before responding.

That is the key. When they need to think back before answering your question, they reveal to you, their thinking style.

They do that with their eyes.

There are 3 major thinking styles. One is not better than the other. We just use the one that is our natural way, to look at things. You care, because you will be much more successful, if you match your presentation and words, to fit how your prospect easily digests information. If we present our story, in a different thinking style, they need to stop and convert it, to what makes sense to them. That does not flow for them as well as, if we made it easy and comfortable for them.

The three thinking styles are:
Visual
Kinesthetic
Digital

When you ask them a thought-provoking question, they will show you which thinking style they use, with their eyes.

Visual

People that are visual, "see" the situation. When they recall, they remember a video, of the event. When they buy a house, they want a view. You would stand on the deck with this buyer. When they shop for clothes they come home with bright colors. You would show this buyer the latest accessories or use of stripes. When they are a corporate buyer, they love to see visuals, colorful presentations and completed marketing concepts, not pencil sketches. Use professional looking materials. When you ask the big, thought provoking question of someone, who has a predominantly, "visual" thinking style, they pause and look up, to recall the answer. Watch their eyes. They look up ,usually off to the right or left, but always up.

Kinesthetic

People that are kinesthetic "feel" the situation. When they recall, they remember, how the event felt. When they buy a house, they feel the family room fireplace coziness and how it feels to bring family together around the kitchen nook. When they shop for clothes, they come home with warm colors and clothing that makes them feel a certain way. Their closet always has less diversity than Ms. Visual. When they are a corporate buyer, they need to feel good about their decision. It is important, to use their comfort words that they use and not overwhelm them with repetitive data and slide shows. It needs to feel right for this "kinesthetic" thinker.

When you ask the big, thought provoking, question, of someone who has a predominantly, "kinesthetic" thinking style, they pause and look down, to remember how that event felt. It is usually off to the right or left as well, but always down. Watch their eyes. They look down before they answer the tough question.

Digital

People that are digital, "analyze" the situation. When they make a recollection, or make a decision, they analyze the facts of the event. When they buy a house, it needs it to make sense. You stress the neighborhood values, ease of re-sell, monthly payment after tax write-off, kids each getting their own bedroom and drive time to school or work. Not fun to go shopping with a digital because they are looking for a bargain or may come home, with nothing. When they are a corporate buyer, it is all data. They relate to graphs and charts and numbers.

Nothing more exciting, than the details of the delivery schedule, to this person. It needs to make sense, to the "digital" buyer. They are very logical and need their questions  answered, so they can check each question off the list, before they move on.

When you ask the big, thought provoking question, of someone who has a predominantly, "digital" thinking style, they pause and look sideways to recall or think through the response. It might be right or left but they will look sideways.

We all, have some of all three styles, in us and we use all three styles of thinking, to make major decisions. Do not insult the kinesthetic buyer, by ignoring the facts or not using visuals. We are best, when we have satisfied all three styles, of our client. Just understand, that one style is dominant and their "go to," process for making decisions. After the kinesthetic thinks it looks OK and the numbers check, back to: "This just feels right."

Do this at the first appointment. Look for reasons to interject a question, that requires thought and watch carefully. That allows you, from the very beginning, to break through a few feet of the ice. If you can figure out early on, how to tweak your presentation and your words and your style, to be in their dominant language......

Boomskackalacka, baby...

I usually start with…

Would the mouse jump on the table,
if the cheese, was on the floor?

Quitters Prosper

(No matter what your mama told you)

This is a fabulous concept. I hope you love it, as much as I did, when I first learned of it.

I liked the idea of it, before I even read about it. I saw a title, "Zero Based Thinking" and I knew immediately, this book's for me. I'm not the best at math, but any formula built around zero.... I can keep up with this one. In grade school, the "zero question", was always the trick question. I am ready, for any zero based multiplication, addition or subtraction they throw at me. A little fuzzy on how to divide by zero, but 3 out of 4, I'm liking the odds.

The theory behind "Zero Based Thinking," is that you need to ask yourself, in many different areas of your life,

"Knowing what I know today,

would I make that same decision, today?"

Some say it a little differently and ask,

"If I was an outsider, looking at this decision, and I now have all the information that you have gathered over time by living this situation, would I choose to get involved today?"

You know where I am headed. **Sometimes quitters prosper.** We are supposed to stand back and look at the decisions that we have made, and put each one of them on trial. That individual, stand-alone decision, knowing everything that I now know, would I choose that again? Would I choose it now, if I was not currently, already, involved in it? Was it a good idea or a bad idea.

We should analyze our career choices first. Think bigger picture, as to what field or industry you are in and is that the right arena, for you? What about the company you work for or the company you started. Would you choose your main task, as your main task, today?

Were those great decisions, in hindsight?

Are they great decisions, moving forward?

Mama used to say "You can't look in hindsight." Nonsense. You not only can, but you must. Of course you can't change the past, but just because you made a hasty decision once, does not mean you have to live with it, forever. Once you figure out that it was not the best choice, change.

I can't even imagine how many recent grads, jump into the job market every year and are excited to get an opportunity. They looked through the classifieds and did some online job searches and this was the best j-o-b they could get, at that time. Soooo, they are supposed to ruin their life, when after only a dozen years they figure it out. O.K., 3 years would have been nice, but deal with it. You still have a lot of life left, so move-on and make a good decision, now. Bad decisions, can be offset, by good decisions.

It is not just the things we chose to do, that were our decisions. We all also know the things that we passed up, didn't have the drive to go after, or just ignored as an opportunity. Those too were decisions, and should be put under the microscope.

Hmmmmm, Not as Tall As I Remember...

Knowing what I now know, should I do it today?

If you are very brave, ask this same question of how you spend your spare time. Knowing what you now know, would you really have spent so many nights in front of the T.V. or down at the bar or cheating on your spouse? Too late to take those back, but with the new approach to decision making, you affirm the path forward, as a new conscious choice. If you now know you shouldn't be doing something, stop. Make a different decision this time.

What Would Donald Trump Do?

This same analysis should be used with our clients.
Aye Yi Yi. Some of these guys drive us crazy. I bet they are many of you that would tell me, "Without my worst 3 customers I would love my job. With them, I hate it. "
What would Donald say to them? You're Fired...
In 1978 I was a young Realtor and hungry. I would work with anybody, and I hoped. everybody. I met an investor, let's just call him Paul, that bought a couple houses with me, sold one and listed a several hundred thousand dollar mobile home park with me. Understand, that the year before, my 1st year in the business, I did 2.5 million in volume and my average house sale that year was $32,000. In my market, it would take me 23 more average-priced home sales, to equal this one mobile home park commission.

Booyah....

I know what you are thinking. You think, I figured out to go into commercial real estate, and lived happily ever after. But noooo,

I had my annual board meeting, by myself, at the beach and voted to fire him. It was fabulous. It was the highlight of my year. This guy drove me crazy. He was a whiner and was never happy, never said thanks and depressed me.... Well, not clinically depressed. However, I would start my day excited and ready to kick butt and after one phone call with, the one we shall call Paul, I had to get out of there and would end up going for a drive, wondering what those college kids were picking in that cow pasture. They seemed to be a lot mellower than I was feeling. (It was the 70's after all, so no judging)

I wasn't quite as dramatic as Mr. Trump, but it was years before the reality show. I called, the one we shall call Paul, and told him I didn't think we were a great fit and it would be in his best interest, to find an agent that would make him happier. If it were today I would have said....

"The one that we shall call Paul, You're Fired."

Be the Donald. Do not be Rodney Dangerfield. Have a little respect. Really. If you have a client, that uses you as a whipping boy, don't do that. When we get abused and beat up, we get tired. If we have to deal with some nightmare customer, and we know they will never change, it can destroy your career and marriage. That is a little dramatic and yet not. The energy sucker client has a lasting effect. You don't get off the phone and say, "I feel great now." No, it leaves you depleted and having less focus and energy, to tackle your real opportunities. It is a huge drain on your other activities. It leads to lower production, getting fired and then your spouse saying he/she never wants to have sex with you again.

As a real estate agent coach, I would hear, "I have so much time invested into this client, that I can't stop now." You know, in for a penny in for a pound. Whoa dare, Pardner. Duh, just because you wasted a lot of time, does not make it a good idea to, statistically speaking, waste a bunch more time.

Cut Your Losses

If you are a real estate agent and not yet in escrow, do not pretend to tell yourself, that you must be getting close and about to get paid, on this one.

Yes, it can be harder to dump a client, when you work for a big company and your problem client, who we shall call Paulette, is at a large account. Even in that case, the same applies. As you gain seniority and street cred, dump this account on the new guy.

There might be a way that you can have an inside salesperson or customer service, play an increasing role. Perhaps, you can settle on changing communication methodology to email, instead of phone. Harder to be nasty all the time, when you leave a paper trail. A driver who makes the delivery, might love the diversity and could go suck up to, the one we shall call Paulette, to lighten the need for as much contact by the one we shall call, You.

For independent sales people in many professions, the same question should be asked of their business model. Within your industry, have you chosen the right niche or way to go, to market. If you like your industry, knowing what you know now, would you take a different approach to your business?

If old Bob, knew everything you know about your business, and how the most successful approached it, would I choose your business or business model today or a different approach?"

We always hear about that inspiring success story of the guy who made it. That guy. He failed a dozen times along the way, but now he hit the big time. It is often told as a story of persistence. They even made up a saying that, persistence pays. Well, maybe that too sometimes, but often the guy was not persistent at all. He was just a quitter.(as his mother-in-law says "Can't hold a job"…. not that, that applies nor do I have lasting nightmares) No, he guy was not just another stinking quitter, he was a Quitter, with a capitol **Q**. He quit more stuff, than most people start. The kids on the playground would have chanted, "Quitter, Quitter, Quitter," but instead he is hailed as a Hero of Persistence.

As these successful people travelled down their career path, they would continually stop and put their past and current decisions, on trial. If they now have enough info., to know it was a bad decision, they made a change. The world saw them as failing, over and over, until they found the right niche and then they were instantly persistent, in seeking success. In reality they were practicing ZBT, Zero Based Thinking and when the answer was obvious, they bailed. Not persistent guys, just bailers.

Put your career decision on trial. If market conditions have changed beyond your control, then switch into an emerging industry or at least one with some business life left in it. (I know a great guy, that had a fabulous and rapidly climbing career at Kodak, who you older folks will remember sold a thing called film. We took photographs with it… and mailed it off for developing)

Don't be the last one at the film factory.

Put your life's decisions, individually, on trial. When you are honest and if the answer is to change, it is easier to do so, because you do it with conviction. Would you recommend that your daughter or son, take this path today?

One of the greatest obstacles to change, is the resistance to change. Duh, but really, we get in a comfort zone, we settle, because it is uncomfortable to do otherwise. We need to internalize, that we should at least make the analysis. Would I choose this, right now, if I was an outsider considering my choices. If it is no, realize, that comfortable feeling, is the #1 factor in making a decision. You just decided it was a bad decision. Are you really going to continue to make a bad decision, after you have identified it as bad. Some will say yes, but I hope ever so slightly fewer of you, after having read this.

I hate to state the obvious, but hopefully, many of you will decide that you are at a spot, that is still a good decision today. Fabulous and your mother-in-law will love you. Take this exercise to tweak your business model. Use it as a springboard to dig deeper within your business and ask the question about details and specific, smaller decisions. Tweak things by analyzing which of your practices, words, delivery systems, marketing pieces, or niches, can be improved upon.

Where should you use a new approach, if you were starting fresh today, with what you now know..

Would you hire each of your current

 employees today? Put 'em all on trial and let the scales of justice balance out where they may.

Customer Service...

You're next....

Today is the zero point, in Zero Based Thinking. Everything starts over from today, ground zero, you just have better data to make your decision now, than when you first made it.

Need a do-over? Call it.

I apologize to many of you, for my other brother Bob. Bad Bob. I promised my mama that I would let him talk, at the end of the chapters. Many of you may choose to skip his segment if you do not like his distasteful humor. I apologize to you. To those of you that see some humor in Bad Bob, you are warped.

Bad Bob

Coach says quitters prosper and he suggested I do a little research on that internet deal. Well, Al Gore may need that kind of stuff but I'm a country boy and I know words mean things. I also am smart enough to know, that I know what I know and so I am always right, if I think I know something.

I ain't looking up no nothing that has it's objective to make me a zero. No sir, I ani't doing zero based and I'm not too sure what they mean by thinking.

*I'm thankful. You must do me this honor.
Promise me, you'll survive. That you won't give
up, no matter what happens, no matter how
hopeless. Promise me now, Rose, and never let go
of that promise.
Never let go.*

Titanic...

Tweaking, will take you to New Highs…

Hi,
My Name's Bob
And.... I'm a Tweaker

There, I said it. Feels good to say the words out loud and to no longer hide that fact, as if it is something I should be ashamed of. I'm not ashamed. Not sure I would describe my feelings as proud, but under the "I'm OK, You're OK" concepts, it is who I am and I will no longer walk with my head down, hoping to not make eye contact, with the inquisitive public. Hoping continually, to avoid said potential inquisitor, feeling emboldened enough to ask me the obvious.... "Are you a Tweaker, or what?" Just the acknowledgement, with a nod to their "Hello," is all it takes for some, to feel they have entered a new, closer and apparently deeper, relationship, and just need to know. "Am I a Tweaker?" I am mad as hell and I'm..... oops. that's another chapter and when you get there we shall explore both definitions of "mad," as they may, or may not, apply to the author....

Before I go on, I'd like to take a moment and address the close-minded few. Those clinging to the past, those of you that will say, I should not encourage tweaking as a way to find happiness or as a lifestyle. I disagree and though I enjoy introducing tweaking to senior citizens, that never thought they would feel such strength again, before their time has come, my real passion, is to get to the youth early on. I like to show them why I tweak and often the first tweak is free. They only need to experience the buzz once and they are hooked. The mind-expanding awareness and the adrenaline flow, that comes when you tweak over and over, will change these open minds of mush forever.

I remember the first time I started down that dark path. It kinda, snuck upon me. You know, I come from a good family. You never would have guessed, I would be the one to succumb. If you happen to live near Fremont, Nebraska, or in any of it's suburbs, such as Ceresco, Scribner or Wahoo, please don't tell my mama.

It was back in 1979. Oh baby, the 70's were something else. Tweaking isn't the only thing we did. I was at a Tommy Hopkins seminar. Man that Tommy could groove, he was a cool cat, not like these slick sales seminar leaders of today. (referred to as the SSS) Old Tommy put on quite a show. I don't have proof, but I am pretty sure when Mr. Tommy Hopkins was on stage, he was tweaking too.

He was something else up their performing and giving us everything he had. Old Tommy told a story about when he started, it was a time back when we wore suits, but Tommy was straight out of high school and only 18 years old. He saved enough money to get his real estate license but he couldn't afford a suit. So, he wore his high school band uniform. He tore off those little things on the shoulders and wore that band uniform, every single day, for 8 months. Young Tommy had a slow start and he would be the first to say it.

Tommy's car wasn't the best. He used duct tape to wrap around the passenger side door post which insured the door would not fly open on corners. It also made it a dash hard to get in and out of that side and the window was permanently open. Fortunately he lived in sunny California.

Tommy tells the story about getting a floor call, from an executive that was flying into town, to look at homes. Tommy picked him up at the airport and as he held the back door, for his new client, he advised "I suggest that you sit behind me. Not quite as windy on this side." Eight months he wore that band uniform. A later, Tweaking Tommy, was something different, at the beginning.

In those formative years, when people asked, "How's business?", he would respond, "Unbelievable." Tommy told us that phrase just described it all. Man, those 1st 8 months in that darn band uniform and that beater car, were UNBELIEVABLE.... He felt it as honest and something he could say, with enthusiasm. To this day, that is how he often responds, to any similar question.

I'm telling you, it happened to me, in an instant. Just like that. (imagine old Bob, clicking his fingers for great emphasis and a fine example of just like that, eh?")

I tweaked

It wasn't premeditated. I did not plan on tweaking. It just happened. I sat there in the audience and I said to myself "Tommy is right." I need an answer to these persistent questions. I need to know who I am at my core…. It would no longer be enough for me to respond "Fine" to an inquiry about how is business. It was not OK when things were good, to say simply "Good." No, no. I immediately, without taking a moment to think of the repercussions or consequences of my actions, took that concept and I tweaked it. Right there in the audience with others all around me, I tweaked, my first tweak. I took his "Unbelievable" and I tweaked it. I made it my own and decided then and there, that when I am asked about how business is or my life or the weather, I will respond
"FABULOUS."
As I expand my consciousness to the outer limits……in the background we hear the whistling of the melody to the Outer Limits…. er..uh maybe that was the Twilight Zone theme. Hmmm, one of the problems with tweaking, is that we tend to forget the source and don't care…
I must be honest, that first tweak felt good and I've been tweaking, ever since. My mom doesn't really know about…. You know… the tweaking. It does seem lately, like she might suspect. She makes little comments like, "Hmmm, that reminds me of a quote from so and so…" *This guy tweaked and it came out …..*

GREAAAAAAT…

That's who I am. That is the essence of how I feel and I do not have to deny that anymore. It was not I, that had thought that first, oh so deep, thought, answering life's timeless question of, "How's Biz?" No, it was Tommy. Tweaking, allowed me to set myself free and to follow, in his footsteps. It is OK to plagiarize, steal thoughts and ideas, while taking credit for the genius, if only we tweak them and make them our own first. There is no shame in being the creative soul, that invented a new business model or path to success, but for a guy like me, it might have taken 7 years to get past this "How is business?" thing. Invent if you want. Me, I'm tweaking.

I have no ego. I believe in shortcuts and increasing the odds, over being haled as a creative genius. And the best part is, they always say everybody that is wildly successful, is a genius anyway. Cool.

I'm telling you, that first "Fabulous" after the seminar, was like the gateway drug. It opened my mind to new possibilities and endless copycat opportunities. I knew then, I would take tweaking to a new level. I would steal every great idea, proven business model or closing script. I would tweak them and then pretend, that I invented them all. After all, I would re-invent each, fine-tune it, to adapt to my personal style, which is kinda, sorta like inventing.

I have been pursuing the ultimate tweak, ever since that moment. I propose that you too might consider being a tweaker.

If you read my stuff, you will see that I have the perfect ideas, scripts, concepts and business models….. for me. They are proven and they work. Do not create. Tweak. Please, take my stuff and tweak it. Make it your own. Steal my ideas and go on a seminar tour, with the tweaked results, that you obviously created. I don't care. Write a book entitled, "Good Fred, Bad Fred." See, you even invented that.

For after all, you might not be "Unbelievable" or "FABULOUS." Only you know. You might find that you are "Marvelous," or perhaps, "Better than I deserve." But be careful, that first tweak will open up the door to whole new potential plagaristic possibilities. (referred to as PPP).

Take, as an example, the chapters you are about to read. I believe in my heart that in 1/3 of the chapters, I created/invented each entire concept and no one else has ever.... Blah... blah... Of course, I am wrong. Successful people all over the world, are doing many similar things. I just don't know that they are doing them, so I take credit, for inventing them.

Hmmm, that does leave the other 2/3 of the chapters... Ok, so I stole a few things from books and seminars, I have attended. At least I tweaked them, before I present them as my own. I'm a tweaker, not a thief. When I can't think of any way to pretend to tweak, I acknowledge the source. Hopefully that won't be too often. Usually my formula is: steal, tweak, claim as my own.

Many of us have heard of the Isaac Newton quote "If I have seen further, it is by standing on the shoulders of giants." I remember someone telling me once that Mr. Newton must have been a nice guy, because he gave such a humble answer, to his accomplishments.

Nonsense, poopy pants. They missed the whole point. He was not professing humility, but rather expressing the secret to his success.

Isaac Newton was a Tweaker....

People have lived before us, and some of them, were successful. Perhaps, we should start there and ask, what did they do and how do we do the same? That is the starting point. If you have to start at the bottom and invent your way up the wealth/success chain, you will run out of time. Take as the new base entry point, the systems and models, the successful before us, already tested and perfected.

Success models can be analyzed and duplicated, where they apply. Just a dash of tweaking, to fit your circumstance.

That is the whole point of this book. It doesn't have to be so hard. I get the whole fierce independence and creative genius thing, but maybe you should save a lot of time and take the RISK out of pursuing wealth and happiness. Most people fail. Some succeed. If you can copy somebody that succeeded, seems like it would increase your odds of a similar result.

As you continue reading, do not try and find the ways one chapter might not apply to your business. Instead, understand it doesn't matter the industry, they all have similar paths to building a monster business in sales. Whether Realtor, corporate newbie or seasoned professional, this book shares ideas and ways to stand out and assure a great career, and not just a great year.

We will look at how to build a database and more importantly how to make it work for you. We will talk about synergy, script concepts and Warren. Successful folks, use group settings for higher returns and design systems that personalize the communications, with their business partners, to reach a deeper relationship. We ask the ever-pressing question, "What Would Donald Trump Do?" and talk about ways to stand out from the crowd. Don't be one possible choice, be the obvious choice. Others have and show us how.

Thank you for joining me on this journey. If you don't benefit from this book, get out of the business. There is no shame in flipping burgers.

Get mentally prepared... before you read this next line, think of the Dr. Pepper song.

"I'm a Pepper, wouldn't you like to be pepper too?")

My names Bob and I'm a tweaker....and wouldn't you like to be tweaker too.... Be a tweaker, yeah you can be a tweaker too...

Bad Bob

I ain't no foo. My mama didn't just drop me on my head yesterday, you know. I have fallen off a bunch of hay trucks and they are bigger than any turnip truck, so you don't foo me.

I know about "Tweaking" and I knew it right away when I saw the title. I told coach I wouldn't read this one cuz my "mama told me not to come...that ain't no way to have fun, son.

That no way to have fu-u-un."

Then he tells me bout some "analogy." I'm not gonna fall for no "analogy" bout nothing. I know what words like "analogy" mean. So what are the 1ˢᵗ four letters of that word, eh? I remember that "ology" means "the study of" & I ain't studying none of that.

Mama also said,
"Remember son, that's how your father got cracked...."

I'm trying to free your mind, Neo. But I can only show you the door. You're the one that has to walk through it.

Matrix

Chapter Four

It Does Not Take 2 To Dance

I believe, we all have an inner artist. Some of us have one that we have let out. Hmmm, I guess you are either an innie or an outie artist.... Life's responsibilities and a host of cultural influences, that I don't want to get into, suppress the dickens out of our natural, artistic side. Instead we plod.

We are not all artists, in the same way. Some people, can draw or dance. Some people, see nature in a unique way and create landscape art. Some folks have a natural ability to see things and imagine them better, if you only..... Some artists have an uncanny knack at understanding what people need and relaying that to them, in a way that they will accept. Some artists create business models that are new and exciting. Many of us have a book or an invention inside of us. Many of us will never let it out.

If you were going to do one, really cool thing, that is a little "out there," what would it be?

What if it worked?

Say there, new guy....
Before you answer the phone,
Take a quick look at this, please.

You are NOT a salesperson

I would like to address an issue that is near and dear to my heart/pocket book. Many of you, take great pride in the fact, that you are a sales person. You are not embarrassed by your closing techniques, or the fact that you wear plaid suits and drive a convertible. You are God's gift to business and nothing happens in business, until something is sold. The world rotates around.... You.

I hope this chapter doesn't diminish your self-esteem. I know that you were all very proud, the day you became a sales person, after the years of required advanced education and the intense residency program.

I know, because I got the memo. It was very exciting and joyous, because what the world really needed, was another stinking salesperson and the collective we, celebrated. There has been quite a shortage of sales people and we are glad to have you. We thank you, for your sacrifice, that few before you have had the inner strength to endure..... to get hired, as a "SALESPERSON."

As an unscientific example, 2 of my golfing buddies are Realtors, one is an insurance man, one sells pharmaceutical products, one sells stuff to retailers and one is an attorney. I would love to replace the attorney. Me, I'm glad to have another salesman in the world, if you are a good golfer. If not.... I'll take the attorney.

I used to be a sales person and did better than most. I used to be proud of my profession and now I am embarrassed. If someone called me a salesman at a party, I would hang my head and shrink home, with my tail between my legs. Another stinking salesperson. I used to be.... You. Bummer.

But, noooo. Dignity regained... I have evolved from Neanderthal Man to Sales Man to Business Man... er... uh.... Owner. Yeah, that's the ticket... I meant Business Owner. When I stopped being a sales person and became a

business owner, my income skyrocketed. I got better control of my life and of my time, and geometrically multiplied the net. You know, that spread between revenue and expenses. If you want to be successful, as a salesperson,

I suggest you not be a salesperson.

Be a business owner.

When I made the transition, I went from B-O-B the Realtor, to B-O-B the CEO, CFO and sales manager, of the Bob Bloom Real Estate Sales Company. For the first time, I stopped trying to sell stuff and decided to run a business, my business. Skip the Rodney deal and treat yourself and your career, with respect. Treat the business side of your life, as a business.

That is kind of a cute statement. I love cute stuff. It sells books. However, what does that really mean? What do successful business owners do?

Running a business of any size, assumes growth and thus hiring employees. No one is about to start hiring people and letting them answer the phone, interact with customers or make any decisions, flying by the seat of their pants. The business owner is going to teach them exactly the words to use and the procedures to follow.

For you see, there is ONE & ONE ONLY, BEST WAY to handle every situation, that might come up. Similar situations repeat themselves, over and over, within your business context. Owners analyze each small act in their business, and decide the best way to handle it. (O.K. you naysayer, critical types.... I can hear you thinking... uh, uh.. there are a million different scenarios and everyone might handle it their way, and blah..blah. You are wrong. Most scenarios we run across, are scenarios that we will tend to run across. Of course, your best way, is different than mine, but we need to, as a business owner would, stop and decide what is the best way we should handle these repeating situations.)

Every business owner has certain protocols, dress codes, procedures and policies. As they grow, they must formalize these procedures, so all may adhere. At that point, they need to write them down, so that they are standard. From time to time, some would be changed, because a better way has been discovered. Then all will follow the new guidelines. When they do this, it forces the owner to really decide the best way, to do things.

Every business owner wants their image to be consistent.

Every business owner holds board meetings. They set aside time, to work on their business, instead of just in their business. At the board meeting, the owner looks at bigger picture game plans and strategies. This is the time to choose long and short term direction, make corrections, analyze the efficacy of your marketing, dream of that perfect niche to develop, decide which clients to dump and which to pursue, and basically, not be so bogged down in the current, that you lose sight of the future.

In my weekly goal setting chapter, I talk about this and in my life, I have a board meeting, that is on my weekly to-do list. It takes me less than an hour. I turn off phones, put my feet up on the desk, (shoeless) and pull out my laptop. I keep a running document, with all my Board Meeting thoughts. This is the time to dream big and create strategies, that would have career changing endings. A weekly board meeting keeps us on track.

Every business owner has scripts and has decided the best way to answer the phone, greet customers, handle objections and solve problems. The best salespeople, all use scripts. They may be scripts that sound a dash different, each time, but they always follow the same multi-step process, to lead the client correctly and thus many of the words, are exact every time. They do this, so that they don't have to think about it and because they took the time to analyze their single best way to handle repeat objections or problems. Never again, leave an appointment and think to yourself, "I wish I would have said such and such." Never again, feel guilty or anxious, about whether or not you lost that piece of business, because you didn't follow-up as good as you do sometimes.

Every business owner analyzes the value of each employee and each activity, that person does. They have to. They need to know, what bang they are getting for their buck, in each area. Whether it is the cost of marketing or the cost of time, what is the return on that investment?

Every business owner delegates. They figure out what they are best at and focus on those things. That also means, that the things that they are not good at, or things, that someone who gets paid less, can do, they pass it off. One way to grow,  is to make more per hour. Dump the low value stuff and spend most of your energy, where you create the most value, for your company. As a business owner, would you have your Rock Star saleswoman, helping out in the mailroom, a few hours per day?

We have all seen the whole team thing explode in the Realtor and Mortgage Lender fields. They brought it to us, but it also applies for a pharmaceutical salesman, the Rubbermaid rep or a Proctor and Gamble newbie.

Every business owner has client touch systems and makes decisions, about how best to "farm," his past clients. He would never send a "thank you for meeting me" note, if it didn't conform to the pre-thought out, perfect way, to say, thank you. Yes, the middle paragraph would vary, because that is where we add the personal stuff. However, each and every time, an employee sends a thank you, after a first meeting, it would cover three main points that the owner has decided, are the perfect things to cover. They are the highest and best practices for that event. The owner might then make the employee, enter that contact into an automatic follow-up system, that takes the human error and whimsy, out of that follow up. Every client gets handled the same way, depending on the category, that they fit into.

When I discuss database development, I say that I believe if you do not have specific follow-up systems in place, for every type of client and every recurring situation you run across.....

STOP WORKING.

Truly. Stop everything and design your systems. It takes too long to think about, what to write and what follow up you should do. Your time is better spent, designing how you will handle every situation, if you were your best, and build your business protocols that commit to protecting that system.

If you are a corporate employee and your company has great systems, so what? Stop and analyze how you personalize theirs or add to it on your own, to develop your brand and unique identity.

Sorry gang, but the world has enough salespeople, perhaps a couple extra. However, the world never has enough good business owners. Running your business, as a business, keeps you on track and gives you true purpose. Purposeful people are more successful. They have a clear direction, that leads them where they chose. They have a better grasp, on the value of their time and the return, on both their time and their marketing dollars.

\

Oh, Man….

I forgot what I was supposed to say…

Bad Bob

Now here is a chapter, I can relate to. I have been trying to tell coach that this is sooooo hard. I don't like to be taken out of my comfort zone.

My mama said that we should develop the gifts that God gave us. He/She, definitely did not give me the gift, of cold calling. I was given great wrists however, and am a natural at flippin' burgers. Sometimes when I'm at the grill and flippin them burgs, I get totally lost in the zone. The flippin' zone, and next thing I know, I have flipped every burger twice. Let the cold-callers try that, eh?

I didn't have time to read the whole chapter, but I suggest you read this title as well. Spend some time and really internalize the title. Make it part of your affirmations, then discover your God-given talents. If you're lucky, we can work side-by-side down at the "Pig n Swig" because "You Are Not a Salesperson.

I'm the G.O.A.T.
No, I'm the G.O.A.T.

You know, Fred,
All of this fightin' and flightin',
Wears me down.
Besides, I'm getting a cold.

Fight or Flight Flipside

We all know, that when we are in a stressful situation, our bodies ramp up, so that we can either fight or flight, right? No, we would be wrong if we thought that.

The amazing human body seeks balance and equilibrium, at all times. When we are scared or stressed, the adrenal gland ramps up. In order to maintain balance, something else has to back off a bit, or entirely. Our entire system can not be running at 110%, all at the same time.

What is shut down, is our immune system. Apparently, our brain has been trained to think, it is more important to fight off the Sabre Tooth Tiger and not worry about getting a cold, during the attack. Good idea, brain.

However, in today's world, the tiger is not our stress creator. It is more likely to be, how to pay our bills, aggressive commuters, dealing with a broken relationship or a nasty old boss.

The problem is, that in the old days, the tiger either ate us or went away. Either way, we no longer need to ramp up our testosterone. Current stress never ends, for some of us. We carry it with us all day long.

Stress, is the initiator of the Fight or Flight Syndrome. Stress, tells our body to ramp up and to shut down and to keep in balance. Stress, ramps down our immune system's efficacy and opens the door to cancer, heart disease, infections, viral illness, depression and …. Let's just go with…poor health.

We need to reduce the stressful situations in our life, or reduce their effects. I'm not sure there are any quick answers, to removing yourself from all stressful circumstances, but dealing with the effects is easy.

We can reduce the effects of stress by:
Meditation
Exercise
Human Touch
Gratitude
Diet

Stress seems anecdotal. People say they "feel" stressed and some folks are "visibly" stressed. But it isn't as if, I have diabetes or high cholesterol, which are measurable. Or is it?

Researchers say that stress is measurable and has very specific effects, on the body. Your body responds to stress, by increasing your heart rate and your breathing. It also releases the hormones adrenaline and cortisol. Under stress, your liver produces extra glucose, to give you that extra boost of energy. These are measurable and thus the amount of stress we are experiencing, as well as the efficacy of stress reducers, can be measured, charted and analyzed. This is not some touchy-feely deal. This is science.

Stress is a killer. We can reduce our stress.

The increased heart rate, raises your risk of hypertension, stroke and heart attack.

The continued release of cortisol, inhibits histamine secretion, which is needed, to fight off viral illness & infections.

The drip-drip of glucose, creates type 2 diabetes.

Meditation
(I'm a big fan)

Really, a big fan. I go through periods, where I meditate daily or so, religiously. When I do that, it has a geometrical effect and is easier to reach a deep state, quickly. For some reason, I get away from it, for awhile and then, I return.

There is a lot of information on the internet, as to "how to" meditate. It is easy to learn, but it takes a bit of practice to learn to shut out, outside stimulus. The best part about meditation, is that it is personalized, and is different for

everyone. There is no right way, so you can play with it.

Besides the full blown meditation exercises, there are a plethora of mini-meditations, that are very practical, to implement into your daily routine. Any little break, that slows down your breathing, relaxes your muscles and clears your mind, is meditation. Just relax, slow down the body and stop thinking about anything. Here are some minis:

Be Present. Feel the air on your skin and hear the sounds, around you. Be intent on only feeling and listening, with no thinking.

Do a body scan. Put your feet up on the desk, close your eyes and monitor your breathing, purposefully slowing it down. Analyze your body, from the top of your head to the toes. Feel tension in each body part and willfully, feel it relax. Then move your focus to the next area.

Listen up. Find some soothing sounds on the internet. Birds chirping or ocean waves crashing, work well. Some people listen intently, to Classical music.

Guided Meditation. Search for free recordings of a guide, walking you through the relaxation process and download it.

Tai Chi. Combine relaxing movements with mind clearing. Five minutes is all you need midday. Find some on Youtube..

Mantra meditations. Get lost in a phrase or couple of syllables. Choose a word or words, that are meaningful to you. It can be religious, nature oriented or purposely monotonous.

Apply heat. Take an electric heating pad and place it on your neck and shoulders, while you sit back and force yourself, to relax.

Have sex. That is actually my favorite technique, but sometimes a little hard to do, when you are sitting at your cubicle, on Tuesday afternoon. However, it has a measurable good effect and much anecdotal evidence. OK, so if that doesn't work maybe just watch some Netflix and chill.

Acupuncture. Get a friend and take turns sticking needles, into each other. I recommend you go first, as the needle poker, and not pokee… LOL …

Exercise

Don't you hate that. Exercise, comes up as the answer, to everything. Next thing you know, I suppose we are

 supposed to eat right. (Yes, reduce caffeine and sugars from your diet to reduce stress effects) Exercise reduces the cortisol in your system and replaces it with endorphins.

(the happy chemicals)

Try and fit some regular exercise routine, into your schedule. In addition, it is beneficial to just get the blood moving, for a few minutes, during your day. Some quickies are:

Sex. (oops… I covered that one already but I did say "quickie."

Get out of the office and walk the parking lot or… By changing your setting and getting the heart up, you will release tension.

Stretching exercises. Slow relaxed stretching, that works out tension, can be done at your desk. Include shoulder shrugs and stretching of the back and neck.

Human Touch

There is considerable evidence, that the effects of stress, are minimized by human interaction with other humans, we like. Happily married folks, have measurably less stress. People that have large and or intimate, social groups, have much less stress. I am not the one to teach you, how to find your soul mate, but here are a few things that can be done easily and will help:

Hug someone. Science shows, that human touch, relaxes us. Kissing, releases happy hormones. Holding hands, is healthy for us. Maybe this is where I mention, that researchers have found that having sex, reduces cortisol levels, in our body.

Call a friend or close relative.
The human interaction of getting lost in conversation, with someone you enjoy, is very therapeutic, for the stressed.

Laugh it off. Laughing has a positive effect, on our body's chemistry, reducing the presence of the bad hormones, and increasing the good. Visit with someone that makes you laugh. I can force myself, to make a fairly genuine laugh by myself, and that is helpful, but combining it with human touch, is preferable.

Gratitude

Once again, I am not making this up. Researchers have documented the beneficial effects, of having an attitude of gratitude. It makes sense. When you are upset and feeling like you got taken, it ramps you up. When we are feeling calm and thankful, our body chemistry responds accordingly. The best way, to incorporate this in to your life, is by establishing a routine of keeping a gratitude journal. It needs to be a regular activity and not one and done. At the end of the day, or as I do it, first thing in the morning, write down in your journal, three things that you are grateful for, during the last 24 hours. You might have to stretch at first, until you get used to identifying all the things in a day, that are good. Don't say the obvious and thus the same thing everyday. This fits into the, strange, but true category. It is true and it forces our brain to look for good, throughout the day.

Diet

I'm really not going to dwell, on diet. We all know what a good diet is. To state the obvious, sugar, carbs, caffeine, lots of alcohol and nicotine are bad for you. Surprise… they also are a factor in the whole stress model.

Bad Bob

Fight or flight, now we're talking. My mama taught me that if a bully knocks you down, get back up n punch him in the nose. I ain't no sissy and I ain't gonna do no flight.

The whole chapter is a little touchy feelie, new wave kinda, stuff, if you ask me.

Meditation? That is like the anti-B-O-B.

Don't just do something... sit there.

My pops tells me, we've got great jeans, so I don't need to workout, to be strong. That part doesn't apply.

I guess the only thing of value in this chapter was the sex part. That might relieve a little stress. Yeah, it's fighting and sex for me. It should be titled
"Fight or Sex."

**Cuz I got good Jeans
I can not lie...
Other salesmen can't deny..
That, I got.. good.. jeans**

Hey, we do what we do best.
We improvise, alright?

Fast and Furious 6

Goin' My Way?

There is no status quo. No coasting, right where we are at. We are either going up, or going down. Our business is either, growing or vulnerable to decline, in its stagnancy. Our marriage is either, going up, or down. We can not say that things are fine and make no further effort, no surprises, growth or excitement, and not have our relationship, be slipping slowly backwards.

In a business world, where change and technological advances are the new norm, coasting, means falling behind rapidly, until our customers, can no longer work with Neanderthal Man. If we are not investing in our message and our delivery system, we will be outspent. It will show.

We must continually, make adjustments, that show our clients that we care enough, to deliver the best product available, to them. We are either, growing or slowly dying.

**Mr.Buffet, sir,
are pre-existing conditions an issue**

Chapter Eight

Warren says....

My roots are in Nebraska. If you are from there, most likely either you, or your mom or grandma, own one or more shares of Berkshire Hathaway. We all know where Mr. B., (only his closest Nebraska friends use that term) lived through much of his life. He was right there, on the busy street with no fence, around his home….and…. if you own a share, or you can drug your mama to sleep and steal hers, you go to the Big Event. Berkshire Hathaway rents out the CenturyLink Center to holds its annual shareholders meeting. That, is a sight to see and worth the price of stock, for admission.

Upwards of 50,000 people will come and go, at the open house, referred to as, the "Woodstock for Capitalists."

All of the companies that are under Warren Buffet's umbrella, show their wares. They display the newest, latest, greatest and probably your favorite item, and sell to the stockholders at great savings. It is more like a festival of ice cream, cowboy boots, candy, furniture and insurance.

Inside the arena, people come and go. Up on stage, sits Mr. Buffet and vice chairman, Charlie Munger. They sit in big comfortable chairs and have a fireside-type chat, with their shareholders/fans. Folks come up to one of the microphones and may ask anything they choose, no restrictions, and the 2 try to answer everyone. They laugh, are relaxed and very thoughtful, in their attitude and responses. Fabulous party, with live entertainment. Sometimes they sit up there for eight hours, if people keep asking questions. Just a lunch break to mingle and back. They are so human and yet so brilliant, that it is a joy to see.

One year I saw a man ask about the effect on the company, if an earthquake took out California. They laughed and joked about it being too warm down there anyway and glad we invested heavily in Nevada. They then explained their diversification strategies and insurances that would handle it just fine….. Surprise.

I saw a tribe of Native Americans come up to the microphone. They were protesting the company's ownership of an electrical dam, that blocked their native rivers. They wanted the dams removed. They were allowed to come up and chant and sing their traditional songs and then say their peace, because the tribe owned a share of stock. The gentlemen on stage were respectful and sincere. (The native Americans have won almost all of those battles against Berkshire Hathaway, at this point. In each the company, not only had to pay to remove their own asset that had been government sanctioned, but in addition, make restoration to the tribes. Costs ran over 30 million per dam and then they lost the revenue stream of those power plants. (I'll bet old Warren choked on that peace pipe.)

And then there was the little girl that shyly, approached the microphone. She looked to be about 13 years of age and looked very nervous. At first her voice cracked and she had to start again. She spoke so softly that the coliseum got eerily quiet. Everyone in the aisles, stopped. She squeaked, " Mr. Buffet, sir, as long as I have memory, my mom has worked really hard to take care of my brother and me. I feel so lucky that she cares so much and we're both doing well in school, but she works two jobs and I know she gets tired sometimes. Sir, if you could give me one piece of advice, to help me make sure that someday, I am in a financial position to return that favor, for my mom, what would it be?

Warren leans forward in his chair and looks her right in the eye. It felt as if 49,999 of us, were completely blocked out, and he was talking directly to her and to her alone. Warren says, " You, are a very brave young lady. The key to your success, will be in your ability to choose your friends, wisely. For you see, we drift in the direction, of the company we keep. The best advice I can give you, is to be very careful with whom you choose to associate."

What do you wanna be, when you grow up?

Bad Bob

Sure. Easy for Warren to say. My best friends, are me. I like a couple of me, but some aren't so fun to be around. I am positive that some of me, aren't on the most likely to succeed, list. Mr. Buffet probably only has a couple personalities. Me, on the other hand....

Growing up in a suburb of Wahoo, Nebraska, I had heard for years about Warren and Charlie's party. I heard it was better than Woodstock, where I stayed for a year, that one week. I just had to go and wanted to talk to him, about how I meet some new friends, those that would go home at night. I promised Mrs. Lee that I would mow her lawn if I could use her stockholder's pass.

I never had so much fun. I ate ice cream until I threw up. Literally. Then I went outside and "scalped" my ticket to a Native American in full headdress. Just hanging around there made me feel like a capitalist. Old Mr. B., rubs off on you. I wonder what the rate of return was on that deal? I never mowed the lawn, ate chili dogs and Blizzards for free and sold my ticket for some fool's gold and wampum.

OOPS.... I forgot to ask about the friend thing.

The wise, accept that the wheel is round,
and run with that knowledge.

Mr. Mellow?

Never seemed too threatening to me.

Chapter Nine

The Mr. Mellow Close

We are all salespeople. Many of us, doing so to earn a living and all of us, try to influence others, now and again. As salespeople, some of us resist doing our jobs. Our job is to get the order and that requires closing the prospect, to get an agreement.

I hear all kinds of excuses for weak and ineffective sales folks, that don't close. I hear:

--- I'm not high pressure

--- I don't want to make them feel uncomfortable

--- They should go home and think about it

--- I work with friends and family

--- I hate to be sold so I know they don't like it either

There is no excuse, for not closing. If you care about the buyer and you have the right proposal, you are a jerk, if you don't help them buy. It is difficult for many people to make a decision. They were taught to be careful and beware salesmen. Great grandpa told them to always go home and sleep on it and they loved their gramps. If you said you would help them, help them. When they are on the edge but need help to get over it, push them.

In some professions like real estate, insurance etc., I believe that if you don't close when you should, that you should lose your license. These poor folks miss out over and again, because you are too incompetent, to do your job. They hired you because they thought you would be a professional and help them get 'er done. Close them.

In the business world, buyers respect and want to work with strong sales people, that have confidence in their product and believe in it enough, to get excited and tell them to buy. There are studies that prove that large corporate-type buyers, appreciate being sold, if it is in earnest. They are not inspired to buy, if the sales rep isn't inspired enough, to get excited and try to close.

I thought I would share with you weak of heart, my Mr. Mellow close:

"John, I have to tell you something. One of my weaknesses as a salesman, is I'm a lousy salesman. Really, I want to be better, but I am just not good at the whole "Closing" thing.

Every year, I have a few clients who miss out on "X" because I was too mellow to tell them, "You know, we should probably do this." They sleep on it and when they call me back and say ____ would be great, it's too late and they miss out. Then I feel terrible. I am trying to be respectful and not pressure people, but sometimes, because I am Mr. Mellow, my client misses out.

I happen to like you and I want to do my job well, for you. Does this happen to be one of those situations, where I am supposed to help you, buy this?

Bad Bob

Coach says to ask a closing question and then shut up. The first guy to talk loses, so I give 'em "the eye" until they break down...

COOL...
Look what happens,
when they come together.

Chapter Ten

Synergize for Success

Thought I would share one of my favorite concepts. It could be a stand-alone seminar, so this is just an overview. I believe understanding synergy and the geometrical effect, it has on a career, is the basis for choosing a career path and then mandatory in developing that path, to it's fullest.

Ever hear of the guy that gets his real estate sales license, but doesn't know anyone in town? He has to start from scratch and make contacts, the old fashioned way. Whatever his previous life experiences, they apparently, brought no value to the table, in developing his real estate business. There was no synergy between his past connections and the profile, of who his current customer should be. If he had friends or family in the area, then some initial synergy, can be tapped into.

Or, how about the Rock Star sales person, that attracted the attention of an up and coming company, that needed help in the sales department. She was wooed away from her current company and brought great sales skills to the position, which is very synergistic. Her former skills, were a base point and she was able to use that synergy and take it to the new company.

However, the new position, was in a different industry and so she received no synergy, from her past contacts. On day one, she had no "ringers," she could call and say "Remember me? I have something, I'd love to show you." It also meant, that she was less educated on the product, than everyone she would call on and so had a big, learning curve. No synergy.

Wouldn't you know, it also so happens, that due to the growth she helped create at the old company, they needed to expand and gave away, what would have been her promotion. That is not very synergistic. Only worse thing could be, is if after she switched companies, they took her out of sales and had her start over as a ... whatever....

Imagine developing a relationship with a big account and treating them like gold, except you are so focused on service that you stop trying to develop add-on pieces of business, to increase order size or getting a foot in the door of a different department. Synergy, needs to be used to make your time increasingly profitable. It means leveraging your business, relationships developed, time spent past and present, and knowledge you have to either:

Get More
Work Less
Have it come easier

The strategic use of synergistic principles, means the difference, between a good career and a monster one. It allows you to have time with your family, for your hobbies and step right back in to sales opportunities, with people that trust you.

One way to achieve synergy, is to not get distracted by activities, that are not synergistic to your BIGGER PICTURE game plan and goals. If we have chosen ahead of time, the type of activities that fit our criteria, then we either pass off to customer service or refer to a peer, for a finder's fee, the business that we run across, that is a distraction to our main focus. If it does not add synergistic opportunities or is not a primary business target, try to avoid spending time on it.

Of course we are pigs and always try to get a new piece of business or get a referral fee, out of every situation. Do not miss those opportunities. However, if your game plan at the beginning of the day, was exciting and filled with purposefully chosen sales or prospecting activities, just say no or pass it off or hire someone to do those for you. Yes, even you corporate sales guys…. You can hire someone outside the company, that you choose to pay for. You can increase your bonus by focusing on the valuable stuff and passing off to cheaper labor your nonsense.

Hmmmmm….

Real estate agents, that run from here to there, and show everything, are out of their minds. Pass off the business that is outside of your focus, for a fee. Spend the extra time developing what will be your bread and butter down the road, the price range and area, that is your ideal market to be involved in. Pass off the acreage property showings and lower priced stuff. Speaking of pigs, also pass off the Luxury Listing appointment with a friend of a friend. That is tough competition, and you can spend a lot of time and perhaps start calculating the commission, while someone that is a Luxury Expert is kicking your butt on their listing presentation. Pass it off to someone, who can probably win the luxury listing competition, if they had the inside track. Go with them and introduce them, or just tell your client that you know the best agent for them. You keep your focus, on your game plan.

Whether it is real estate or corporate sales, if you can establish yourself, as the expert in that area, whether it be geographically or product/customer type, you will be seen as the obvious choice instead of one of the possible choices.

What if you chose to usually meet clients at the same restaurant, perhaps a locally owned place, that would know you and welcome you, when you entered? They would give you better service and make you look important, in front of your client. You gotta love the old, " I have your favorite table for you Bob" deal. That adds a dash of synergy and if you are in an industry where someone who works at the café could give you business, you have added more synergy to that situation.

And how about this: what if you had back to back appointments, at the same restaurant. It would give you credibility, to have each appointment, see that you are busy. Try to have the two clients have something in common, so that you can introduce them, when they cross paths at your table. Have the staff trained how to handle the arrival of the 2nd appointment. Great synergy and extra benefits, compared to having a couple meetings, at 2 different Starbucks. Don't use a bar for the meeting spot. The whole "Norm" deal, from Cheers, is not the image I am designing for you.

In corporate sales situations, consider meeting down in the cafeteria, if the meeting is not a closing type appointment. If you are just meeting for other reasons, try and let everyone see you there and know, you are a vendor on the inside. You don't know who will be a potential add-on piece of business. When calling on larger companies, you also can set back to back appointments in a conference room or the cafeteria etc., so multiple buyers will see that you are with their peer.

Part of the Synergize for Success concept, envelopes the question of how do I take this stand alone activity, that I have to do anyway, and get more business out of that or because of that. Who is a similar client that would respect me, for having this piece of business?

If we have a cajillion, stand alone pieces of business, we can have a great life. If we can use our efforts to be a magnet for additional and much easier to acquire business, our life can be easier and more profitable per hour. Like your mama always said… Great, Greater, Greaterest!

Who is your "ideal" client or customer? Where are they located, what service or product do they buy and how do they interact with their sales partners? How big of a potential account, are they? Make sure, that the majority of your focus, is in trying to develop that group of, "ideal" customers," so that you can have a fabulous life, calling on the segment of your choosing. Hmmmm got that part? Of your choosing…..

WOW
One is Bigger

What if the potential client is a referral from one of your best customers? Do you service them, out of respect to your monster client…. Nah… you don't. What you need to do, is find an alternative, that you feel good about telling the referrer, that here is the best solution possible, for your friend. Because I take your referrals seriously and I commit to helping each of them, to the best of my ability and knowledge, I have referred them off to so and so, who is a specialist in that arena or to my in-house team. I could be a commission pig and sell them myself, but truly, I have found them someone, that can represent them better. I will monitor the sale… or not.. whatever. Just make sure you are being honest and that you have found them someone who cares and will try and represent them, and thus you, well.

As real estate agents, we sometimes are forced to hold open house in the early stages of our careers. The question is how do we achieve some synergistic benefit, from wasting those 3 hours? We need to change our perspective from, "I am holding open house today" to, "I am working for awhile today, at least 3 hours and have a game plan, as to how I best can capture some business, during that time frame." Perhaps the BIG PICTURE sales person, uses the open house time, to add 3 people to their database. It is easy to get neighbors and people that are not serious buyers, to agree to letting you mail them your newsletter and thus assure a great future. You can not control if you meet a fabulous buyer that walks through your door, but you can control if you add some people to your database. It is easy to meet new database folks, if we have a purpose, to meet them. While we hold open house, we have purpose to open a conversation, without being some weird, stalker, door knocking, call the police on, kind of dude. By changing the goal, to what we can control and what would benefit us down the road, that makes, what could be considered an unproductive afternoon, into a Boomshackalacka… 3 new families in my database. Next year is gonna be big. Create huge synergy from an otherwise unproductive open house.

You only have so much time. How do you make it, so that the thing you do today, will make it likely you get more business, in the future, either from the same client or because this activity increases your odds, for a different piece of business. How do I get this sale, to add credibility to me, so that I am the obvious choice in my next sales presentation, to a similar or connected prospect?

I could care less about helping you have a great year. My focus is on creating great careers, thus lives.

Boomshackalacka, baby.

Go through your database and really analyze, "What is it I could do, that would be valuable or nice, for each of my biggest clients and prospects?" Some, one-thing, that is above and beyond. It might be a service for the business you have or it may be personal. Is there something, they have interest in, that if you did … whatever… that they would say, "Wow, cool. That was really nice. I love…." Do they like a sports team, to garden, cook, listen to free music or interested in the local history? Find something that matches up with their interest and they would find interesting. That is taking advantage of synergy by having the knowledge, of what they like and using it to cement your relationship, to a deeper and more personal level.

Do I know two people, that could benefit from knowing each other? Introducing them to each other, uses the synergy of information and relationships, to help the people that might be able to give us business now, or in the future.

It is not all take, take, take. Can you figure out a way, to get your clients a new piece of business or valuable business contact?

Don't just refer them introduce them. If you can help their business grow, they will want to help build yours, as well.

To maximize all aspects of synergy, bring your clients together for a party or gathering that would be fun.

One that:

Creates a reason to continue to do business, in order to be invited again next year.

Shows off you're A-list of impressive clients. People love to work with successful people, so show off your best clients.

Helps build relationships, stronger than just work.

Builds relationships 2 or more levels deep. Having a client that likes your other clients encourages them to like you...

Lets clients that like you, tell each other, how great you are.

What are your personal interests and what is fun for you. Find potential clients that love the same thing and do it, with them. Get to know each other, while sharing your passion and then, do business later. Do you have a local sports team, that you follow? If so, I am sure you have several clients, who also love them... the nature of sports, eh? Invite several of your clients to a sports bar, to watch the game. It brings together your clients and assures they enjoy your time together. That is synergy. Enjoying your favorite team, and getting more business as a result. Boomshackalacka.... synergy.

In some industries, we have our inner circle. People that we give business to, that help us, in ours. We have choices, but use this delivery service, painter, handyman, computer guy, etc., over another. It is very synergistic to go to them and let them know that your new minimum entry

Raise Expectations

point to do business with you, is to give you at least one referral, per year. Doesn't apply to every industry, but more than you first might think. If someone is vested in your success and you're contributing to theirs, expect business in return.

Synergy can be insured by the development and nurturing, of your personal database system, or CRM if you prefer. It is critical for corporate sales people, as well as independent businesses like Realtor, insurance, automotive sales, mortgage lenders....ad infinitum.

The corporate world, is full of opportunity and yet sometimes, events or relationships beyond control, keep your career, stifled. The only way up, is either out and up or out, then up. You need to build your personal relationship management system, that includes people such as: your clients and all the folks you see and recognize while visiting that client, your competitors, other vendors that call on your clients, your friends and family and service people that you interact with regularly.

You would keep track of: names and contact info. Such as phone, email etc., products they purchase, what their hobbies are, do they have children and what do you know about them, what is their biggest challenge, favorite sports team, what state from, college attended, and on and on.

It doesn't matter that you have a fabulous CRM, you use at your work. If, it is owned by the company, you must develop yours, on your own, in order to assure you never lose synergy, by having to start over. Nothing worse than getting laid off, or choosing to leave, and not having all the data, to assure a smooth transition to your next venture.

In addition, in your personal CRM, you can make notes that you can not keep, and are sometimes illegal to keep, on the

company computer. I am talking about data such as, if they are married, how old are they, what is their faith, etc. If you know that a client's a Christian then you should send them Christmas cards that say, Merry Christmas not Happy Holidays. With your own data, you'd send a happy anniversary card to a married person, email a thank you note to a veteran on Veteran's day, ask about how their dog "Spot" is doing, or call them up before the ball game, of their favorite team. You build deep relationships if you find things that are meaningful to them, to talk about. Because we have so many conversations in a day, month, life... we forget some of the small stuff. If we start over with, do you have a dog, when we asked that a year ago, we lost the advantage of synergy created, by being able to look up personal information, before every appointment/interaction.

How you get synergy, is by fully using every conversation as a building block, for a stronger and deeper relationship. If you forgot she had a dog, you can not build on that knowledge by starting the next conversation with "how is Spot doing?" And when she responds how he has been acting up.... You enter that, into the system and on the next call, you start at even deeper level and ask "Is that darn Spot still acting up?"

Unless you have a photographic memory, it has great value to keep notes on people you care about   (Wouldn't it be nice before Thanksgiving dinner to look up old Uncle, what's his name and recall his favorite, whatever...) as well as knowing that you will have forever, a personalized collection of data about everyone you have met in a business setting. They will think you are brilliant, if you just recalled that you met 3 years ago, at that sales seminar in Wahoo and you knew she had a daughter, that was attending the University of Nebraska. You are instantly at a deeper level when you can start at the level of "How's that Cornhusker daughter, doing? Man, they have the best football team in the world, eh?"

The same applies to the ever-dull, corporate trade shows. Since you have to go, attack them with a strategy that develops your long-term career, as much as chasing short term. Try and meet additional buyers from the same company, as your clients that you see, bring together buyers that are in the same industry or similar, introduce people that have similar hobbies, meet your competitor to see if they are dumb enough to say the wrong thing or to let their management see you in action, in case they are hiring down the road. Look for new opportunities and trends. Decide how best to use your time, ahead of time, to utilize every precious moment that you are not in the booth. When you're on the airplane home, skip the complimentary beer and write some hand-written notes, to the people you interacted with. Yes, the potential customers, your competitors and folks you met at the peripheral of your world. They will be shocked that you wrote, because they know there is no immediate business for you. They will remember, in case you two shall meet again. Either way, you will.

Synergy is created, when you get an extra bump from an activity, you were going to do anyway. If, you are headed to a trade show,.....yawn .... ask your best clients that are not going, if they have any product they would like you to try and spot for them. It creates synergy in three ways,

First: It gives purpose to your initial call to the client, it gives them a reason to anticipate your return and another phone call and then an interesting meeting when you show them what you found. The synergy added to the 2nd and 3rd contact makes them much more impressionable.

Second: The genuine effort you made, and the rare chance you found them something, will create a lasting (I say synergistic) effect, on your relationship. People like to return favors. No quid pro quo, just the way most of us are wired. We are more open to helping out someone, who has helped us in the past.

Third: Enter into your database, the people that you meet while looking for your client. If you help someone get a piece of business, they may later be a good employment option. They will remember you, if you remember them. Send them a thank you email just as if they were the one doing you the favor.

On a similar note, we have all heard that it is important to give, to get. We receive more, when we are looking out for the other person and not reeking of commission need and tainted advice. I didn't invent that. There is great value, in helping our clients solve problems, that do not involve a sale, with us. (Bummer, I definitely didn't invent that)

The synergy is even greater, if you are able to connect two people from your personal database. One plus one does not equal two in this whole geometrically multiplying, synergy deal. Bringing two people together, that you do business with or care about, not only do they both appreciate it, but they get the opportunity to re-affirm how cool you are to each other. You gotta love it, when you hear one client say, "Thanks Bob, you are always the best," in front of another client.

BOOMSHACKALACKA, BABY....

I hate to sound like a pig, but this book is about being a monster, not just good. If bringing two people together has synergy, how about 3 people or dare I say 7 people. What the heck, let's dream big... how about I figure a way to bring together 100 potential, clients.

What do your clients like to do? If some like to listen to free music in the park, be that guy that goes 2 hours early and sets up a group of chairs, in the best spot. Let your clients know, that if they get stuck in traffic, no problem. You got their back and they can slide in at the last moment and have a great seat. You can buy those folding concert chairs, for under $10. So get a dozen and bring together some of your clients.

If you have a local football team that many support, be that lady that goes 4 hours early and gets the best tail-gate location. Invite all that are going to the game, for your specialty, baby back ribs and a cool one, before they go into the game. You don't even have to be a big sports fan. Just be a good cook (or know one) and party on. Everyone is happy, upbeat and fun, before the game. What a great time to have a quick social contact and introduce hard core fans, to each other.

I have a separate chapter about group meetings but understand that one plus one plus one plus one plus one plus one plus one is….. a bunch in my world of…….

You thought I was gonna say "Synergy" again didn't you?

Bad Bob

Tired Creepster, apparently…

Bad Bob

Synergy, shmynergy, what a bunch of nonsense. Old coach has some good ideas but doesn't really think through all of them before he tries them out on me.

I tried this synergy deal out and think I'll go a different direction.

I tend to be a night owl and love to go on long walks in the middle of the night. I wear all black and stay in the shadows so I won't scare anyone. I synergized that with focusing on developing a niche with first time buyers. Many of the first time buyers are also up late at night. You can find them downtown at the dance clubs, so that is where I went.

I wasn't going to pay any cover charge, so I hung around outside the clubs and when the young ladies came out, I asked them if they were interested in looking for a new place to live with me?

Apparently synergy is creepy. I heard a lot of "Creep" "Creepster" and things like " Get out of here, creepy old guy."

Coach means well but......

We all seem alike,

Unless, you tell 'em otherwise.

Tell 'em You're Great

As you may know, I started as a real estate agent, then real estate agent coach then…. Whatever this is. In this next lesson, allow me to first speak in Realtor terms but trust me, it applies to sales people across the board. I will bring it back around but use your imagination to put it in your specific context.

Our clients, whether they be the stressed out business owner that never gets out of the office, or the buyer for a large chain that never gets out of the office, or a family that needs to sell their home, they all think that we are overpaid. We are those high commission folks, that get company cars, take clients to lunch, golf and pretend it is business, and basically are Primadonnas that have it way easier than the buyer of our services. We even get out of the office and get to drive around while others are chained to a desk.

In the case of the real estate agent, all that the client sees is, us open a few doors, gloss over some paperwork and get paid a bunch. It looks fun. Why do you think everyone thinks they want to be a real estate agent…. Before they try it?

The reason is, that we make it look too easy. They don't see, what we really do and have no idea, what hoops we jumped through and the genius, that we exhibited…… unless, we tell 'em.

The same is true in the corporate sales setting. Our clients have no idea, of the off hours we put in or the time away from our family. They have no idea that we just spent the last of our political capital convincing the boss to get the special pricing that we gave that client. They have no idea of any of it….. unless we tell 'em.

Countless Realtors, after a difficult negotiation, call their client and say, "Congratulations. You got the home."

Countless times the corporate guy, that worked his tail off to bring together the delivery on time, coordinating special overnight shipping from Fremont, Nebraska and then having a driver make a special run, all the while beating up the manufacturer, for special pricing, says "Your order made it on time. Thanks a lot. We appreciate your business."

What A Waste

If you perform a miracle, more importantly, if you don't, let your client know how hard you worked for them and what a hero you are. Before you tell 'em the good news, walk 'em through a dramatic story, of how you created magic and got them what they desired. A real miracle worker and frankly, they should feel lucky to work with you…. The Magic Man….. or Woman, as it so may be.

You may think that the way we deserve a big fee or loyalty, from a large account, is if we have value, beyond price. You would be wrong. The way we deserve a monster fee or undying 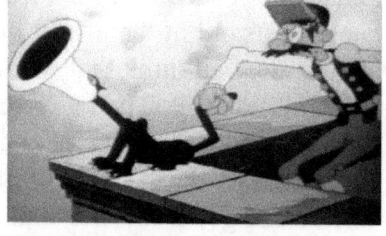 loyalty, is if the client REALIZE,S we have great value. Who cares what we do, if no one knows and they assume, that it was no big deal. If we get them their price reduction, an amazo delivery, on a one time order, or their home sold at top price, they will think it is no big deal, if we act like, it was no big deal. They may even come to see that as the new standard, instead of being appreciative. Tell 'em what a big deal it was.

As a Realtor you might say something like " OMG, that seller is a tough one. He knows he has great property and there is a lot of interest, from other buyers. The listing agent told me, she expected more offers by tomorrow, so I pulled in a favor and got Susie, who I have known for years, to push it through tonight. I feel very fortunate that I have worked with this agent so many times, over the years and she said she knew, if I was involved that it was a solid deal, so she left her kids soccer game early, for you.

By the time she got back to her office, she already had another offer. I don't know if it was better or worse, but I am so glad I have a good reputation, with this agent and yes, congratulations, we got your home, by minutes. What a great

home. I am so glad we snuck in before all the competition created a bidding war, that I really wanted to avoid for you guys.
Congratulations."

Now your client thinks you are a hero. If you would have called and said "we got it", they would have thought to themselves, we should have offered lower. Feel that difference. Hmmm, they accepted the offer. No big deal, I must not have negotiated well

enough to Whoa… I am so lucky, I picked El Bobbo as my Realtor.

Catching how that applies in the corporate world? If you just let them know you got their price reduction without the drama, they will be more inclined to think they should try again instead of … Whew….We got away with one there. My sales guy, really tries hard for me and I am appreciative.

Don't over do it, but realize that this is not just for the big things. If you get a special delivery, bring in a new item, get special pricing, fix this or do that, let them know that it was not just standard and that you care about them enough, to go the extra mile.

They will be more appreciative and thus loyal. Trust me, if you don't tell 'em you're great, no one will.

In the "one last thought" category: when a customer thanks you, never say no big deal or shut them off early. Let them go on, until they stop and then acknowledge that, this was a tough one and you were really glad for the outcome and…. You're welcome.

In the 'thought after the last thought,' category: When someone is thanking you and thinks you are the best, it might be the right time to say **"You are welcome, do you happen to know of anyone else that might benefit from the way I work?"**

"You are welcome,

do you happen to know of anyone else

that might benefit, from the way I work?

Bad Bob

This chapter has been life changing for me. I didn't know I was great until coach told me. He said that only about 10% of Realtors answer their phone and that almost none of those hold open house. I figure, if I just answer my phone while I am at an open house, I will be in the top 2% of all agents.

Tell 'em I'm great? Absolutely. I decided to make that my marketing campaign. "Top 2%" of all agents. Because I am not stupid, I know that pithy quotes should be short and memorable so I changed it to "Top 2" of all agents. Work with #2 or you are too little and too late."

Thanks coach. After all my hard work and dedication, it feels good to have made it. Maybe I should lease a Porsche.

Not a Very Big Number

The 3 Rituals for Success

I'd like to talk about three, 5 minute Rituals, that if implemented into a salesperson's life, assures consistent improvement in their numbers (income) as well as in their personal, sales skills.

Whatever you do, don't stop any of the rest of what you are doing. Do not stop all of your prospecting and follow-up activities. I am not suggesting that 15 minutes a day, is all you need to do... come on now, don't even think about it.

BUT... if you want a boost in your income, I have an easy answer.

The three, 5 minute time frames, when we do our rituals are:

> **First 5 minutes of your work day**
> **5 minutes before a big appointment**
> **5 minutes after the big appointment**

First 5 Minutes of the Work Day

I love to read great books. Literally, not on a device, just printed out and I hold it, in my hands. That allows me to highlight and dog ear pages and keeps me from sucking my thumb.

There are several good ones, that talk of how we need to find, our Big Why. We need to have a monster goal that would "change lives for the better," kind of goal. Really imagine your best life you could have, and most fulfilling contributions we could make, to the world, and to your family. What would be an off the charts, fulfilling life for you? Identify your BIG WHY and what would be a huge goal and life, for you to have. The thing, that would excite us everyday, to work on. The thing, we would talk someone's ear off about.

Then we work backwards and figure things we could do in the short term, which would point the nose of our ship in that direction. Make a list of little things you would need to do to assure that you are slowly headed that direction, towards Your One Big Why PurposefulThing

Now here comes the Ritual, every morning, for the first 5 minutes, if needed, 15 seconds if not needed, when you get to the office, decide what is the one thing, just one little thing, you could do today to continue down the path towards your biggest goal. Got it? Just one thing, that is step towards a really big life, so that we never go a full day, and do nothing (aka: no-thing), towards our biggest ambition.

Which Step

Do I Take First

Commit to doing just one thing today and then time block it into your schedule. Literally, write in your schedule or calendar, when you're going to do it. Then, go about your day and do what you need to do. Don't move that appointment. Treat it like your number one most important thing, to accomplish today. Everyday do one thing that takes you, with baby steps, towards your dream.

5 minutes before a BIG appointment

So often in our career, we are juggling many balls at once. We are fiercely proud of the fact, that we talked on the phone and solved a few problems, while driving to our next appointment. We get there and just go in and wing it, because we are pros. But really, we are a little distracted and have a million things on our mind. We're more likely to miss that point, we meant to bring up, if we go straight from one task to an important task. I propose, that before you go inside, that you sit in a quiet place and totally clear your mind. Do a mini version of a meditation and focus on your breathing and a lack of thoughts. Force your mind to think of nothing, except the monitoring of your breathing.

Author of The Charisma Myth, Olivia Fox Cabane, tells us that before we speak or sell or present, we should stop and put our minds in a place of gratitude and love and acceptance. It will show in our eyes and the client will feel it. We need to remind ourselves that the person we are about to meet is a good human and that, skip the whole commission thing, we would really like to help them and have a positive effect, on their lives. I recommend that before any big appointment or important event, you stop and either read or say to yourself, an affirmation similar to the one, I have written here. It should go something like:

--I am looking forward to seeing _____ today. It is a gift that I get this opportunity to help them. One of the great things about this world, is how everyone is so unique and different, from each other. I have not walked a mile in my clients' shoes, but I know their path, was different than mine. Their childhood, relationships and work experiences, all influenced them to be who they are. Please, help me to not judge them, if they react differently than I would. My life has been different than theirs. I am no better than they are and God loves them, just as much, as God loves me. I hope that as they go forward, that they have a fabulous life, which gets better and better.

I accept _____ for who he is and will give 100% of my attention to him. If I really focus on every word he says, I know I will better understand and know him. If I find my mind wandering, I will bring it back, so that he will know I am really listening and that I care about him, because I do.

I can see myself being very relaxed and professional. This is a very comfortable conversation for me. I will say less and have pauses before my speaking, to give time to reflect. I am the best and my product is the best, for them and I am very fortunate to be here, regardless of the outcome. I am grateful for an opportunity to share my skills and be the best rep for _____ to work with. I am very fortunate to have a job that allows me to help so many people. I am thankful that I have been given the natural skills, to be able to be in the moment and to have empathy, for all people and to calmly understand the words I should use, that will help them realize, that I really am the best company for them.

Got it? Center yourself and bring your focus in on them, while keeping in mind, that you come from a place of gratitude and acceptance. It doesn't mean we give up and don't close. It means we commit to understanding and respecting them. Their opinions are valid and if I had lived in their shoes, I might think the same.

We still try and help them and we close them, if we know we are the right thing for them. But we do so with respect. When you reach that place of calm gratitude and confidence, stop and review your notes before you go in. Make sure you cover each point and deliver your message in the order that you designed, without getting side tracked.

5 Minutes after the BIG appt.

In the sports world, all of the greatest athletes, have a post game analysis. They watch tape of their performance and evaluate what they did well and what could be improved. What you may not realize, is that many of the Monster Salespeople, do the same thing. Many of the big team leaders do the same thing with their team members.

The road to constant improvement, travels through the place of continuous self-analysis, and the tweaking of our words, actions, and our responses.

It doesn't do us any good, to leave and think that the seller is a bum and stupid, because he chose a different option. That is totally outward centered, and feels good to some of us to place blame elsewhere. If we want to improve our closing ratio and have more success in the future, we should stop immediately after our appointment, while it is still fresh in our minds, and ask ourselves, what did we do great. Write it down, to make sure you emphasize that segment in the future.

Just as important of course, is what could we have done differently, or better. How could we handle that situation differently, next time. Do we need to develop a new script for that repeating objection? Write it down and contemplate, how we  might continue on our path, of consistent personal growth and higher closing ratios.

This is meant to become a habit, that we form and do after every major appointment, whether it was a great one and we got the business, or if we failed and did not get the business. That 5 minute time frame, will become invaluable to you, in identifying what is needed, to make sure we win more often.

Sounds easy, doesn't it? Duh, it is easy. Three times a day, take 15 seconds to 5 minutes, and change your career. Really, change your life.

1st Ritual.. Can you imagine how much MORE LIKELY you are to achieve your greatest and wildest dream if you actually take some step in that direction everyday and do at least one thing?

2nd Ritual.. Can you imagine how much better some of your appointments will be, if we don't just race in, coming straight from being on a phone call, solving problems on a different transaction. Our attention will be refocused and our emotions will be brought in check, so that we can be 100% present, with the client that is in front of us. They will feel it.

3rd Ritual, we can't improve our closing ratio if we keep doing the same thing, we did last time. The only way to improve, is to stop and reflect on what was fabulous and in what area, we would like to have a do-over. Because in life as a salesperson, we really do get a ton of do-overs... just not on the client we just lost.

We will have the same or similar situation, come up again and again. That, is our do-over, to commit to ourselves to handle things slightly differently next time we get the similar opportunity.

I'm feeling that is worth a BOOYAH.

As Burt & Ernie might say…
One of these things is not like the others…

Bad Bob

So, I just scanned this chapter, but coach says I catch on fast. *** I read the highlights and I get it. To be a successful salesperson, I need to spend 15 minutes a day of focused work. It just has to be at the right time of day. The best part is that if I don't have any appointments that day, I only have to work that 5 minute shift at the beginning of my day. That would allow me to get a dozen more sales jobs with all my extra time. Imagine how much I could make if I spread around my focus to 13 different things.

AHAAAAA…. I get it. This is that moment. I clearly see my path to riches. Diversification and lots of it. If I'm O.K. and you're O.K., then I deserve to be rich. I just need to have several jobs of a decent income and then I don't need to be successful in any one. Just give 'em each 5-15 minutes a day.

Boomshackalacka, Baby…..

*** That is true. I do catch on fast. Sometimes coach only needs to spend 2 or 3 minutes with me for the hour of coaching I pay for, cuz he says I'm such a fast learner.

To Phone   or   Not To Phone

That is the Question...

To Phone or Not To Phone

To phone or not to phone, that is the question
Whether tis nobler of the mind to suffer
The slings and arrows of outrageous prospects.
Or choose to drown in a sea of busywork

To phone or not to phone, that is the question
Perhaps, we phone no more and die a salesman's death
To nap. To sleep perhaps to dream, but there's the rub
For in that nap of death, the dreams may come
Oh to stop, the dreams of success unachieved
The nightmares of a wasted life persist

To phone or not to phone, that is the question
Destined to grunt and sweat under a weary life
Where fear has made a coward of your soul
Or take a stand against mediocrity
And do the thing that's hard, almost too much
And thus by so doing, achieve your best

To phone or not to phone, that is the question
A silly man sits by the phone and waits
Perchance to hit the phone-in lottery
While a simple man picks it up and dials
To dial. To dream of calls answered with glee
Prospects waiting for someone to call, Alas

To phone or not to phone, that is the question
                    Duh, dial it.

That felt good...
Thank You for the Opportunity,
To say Thank You

Chapter Fourteen

Thank you
Same Words but Why

I would like to visit about saying thank you, to our clients. The, when, why and how, of saying thank you, in a professional setting.

Now come back here, don't tune this out yet. This is not going to be what you think. You may think you don't need to hear this, because your mama taught you all about having good manners. I am going to take a different approach and reference some interesting research.

Why

Let's start with why. This is the most obvious part of the equation. Our mama's taught us, that it is good manners, to say please and thank you, and you don't want to disappoint your mama now, do you? Huh??? OOPS... my bad. I joke, yet I don't. We know down deep, because that is how we were taught, that thanking people, is the right thing to do. If we don't say thank you, we are actually going against our grain. If we told our mama, we would say thank you and we don't, we are not treating ourselves with great integrity.....the infamous, slippery slope.

But there is much more to it than that. People like to be appreciated. Some days it feels like there are approximately 2.6 million salespeople in the county of 250,000 residents that I live in. I don't care if you live in Wahoo, Nebraska or New York City, there are probably more salesmen and women, than there are folks that live there. People have a lot of choices and they know it.

But, they have chosen you to work with. I believe it is imperative, to acknowledge that, to your clients... and I am not talking about "thank you" as you are leaving. I believe you should, at some point in the conversation, stop and make a real point of acknowledging, that you realize they have many choices and you really appreciate their business. I tell them that I am honored to represent them, because that is true.

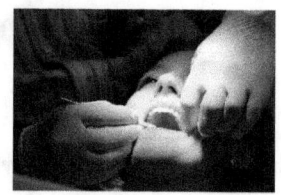

The same applies to thanking people that give us referrals. If you would like them to give you another referral sometime, you need to reinforce their behavior, which encourages them, to repeat it. Why do we thank people.

Why

Because it is the right thing to do and because it reinforces their behavior, so that it feels good to them, to repeat the behavior.

Adam M. Grant & Francesco Gino published their data on this segment of gratitude, in The Journal of Personality and Social Psychology. In their studies, they asked people for help and thanked some and did not thank others. They found that the participants, who were thanked, were more willing to provide further assistance. Indeed, the effect of 'thank you,' was quite substantial: while only 32% of participants, who received a follow up request for assistance without having been thanked, did so, the number of people willing to help went up to 66%, if they had received a simple thank you, previously. That's a 100% increase in willingness to help, just for doing what your mama told you to.

Many of us live in a referral based business. When we are fortunate enough to identify people that are referrers, we develop that relationship, thank them and make it feel good for them to help us.

Many of us are in a business where our buyer has choices, besides our company or product. When we are fortunate enough to win one of the battles, develop that relationship with the buyer, thank them and make it feel good for them, to help you..

The third reason that we should say thank you, is that it

makes us feel good. Literally. In the relatively new field of positive psychology research, gratitude is strongly and consistently linked to greater happiness. Expressing gratitude helps people feel positive emotions, relish good experiences, improve their health, deal with adversity, and build strong relationships. This is not one of those deals where I explain to how that works. Let's just go with the research and say "cool."

Studies were done by psychologists, Robert A. Emmons from the University of California, Davis & Michael McCullough from the University of Miami and Martin Seligmann from the University of Pennsylvania.

In summary their research shows, if people either wrote thank you notes, or kept a gratitude journal, in which they wrote what they were grateful for daily, they reported a 25% higher happiness level, had fewer visits to the doctor, were more optimistic, exercised more, had better and longer sleep and reported an improvement in their personal relationships. That's a lot of good stuff for just saying thanks, or by daily, contemplating your good fortune.

What is really interesting to a "show me" kind of guy, like old B-O-B, is that not only do we now have anecdotal information, reported by the test subjects, but researchers have measured and found proof of the effect of having an attitude of gratitude. (hmmmm, I like that… attitude of gratitude) They found physical evidence, that supported their theories, with a variance in cortisol levels, reduced stress, heart rate variabilities and even increased activity in the prefrontal cortex.

Did you get that? There is anecdotal as well as measurable, scientific evidence that shows that if we learn to say thank you and if we write thank you notes and/or create a daily gratitude journal, we will be healthier, happier and have an improvement in our personal relationships. Cool…. And sooo easy.

When

When: Immediately and often. Really. When we get a referral or a purchase order, we don't wait until we get the listing or deliver the product. We give the referrer/buyer the immediate gratification, of thanking them immediately and letting them know we appreciate it (I say honored). We then reinforce it by thanking them and updating them on the progress. Don't over do it, but people love to get an update when the special order ships or the referred client closes, on their new home. That's how we reinforce the behavior and encourage them to do it again, sometime. We make them feel appreciated.

In today's cell phone addicted world, it is a great idea to text or email from your cell, a thank you for your time and nice to meet you and I will get back to you as soon as I get the info I told you about…moments after you leave a client. Second: There are mobile apps such as thankyoupro and thankyounote that you might check out, that will assist in that.

Third: I believe that we all should carry in our briefcase, thank you notes, so that we can pull over right after an appointment and write it and drop it in the mail on the way back to the office. In most communities, there are mail drop boxes that have a last pick up between 4:00 and 5:00 P.M., and if we get it in the mail by then, your client will receive it the next day. Readers, listen to me…. Clients are not surprised if they get a thank you note… though most sales people don't ever make the effort… but they are shocked and impressed if they get it in the mail less than 24 hours after they met you. It will really set you apart. Yes. Some cities are 2 day, but the point is the same. Get it in a mailbox, close to the client's office and quicker is better.

How

How: An in person Thank You is best. People appreciate you making the effort to come see them. Also most people love to get mail.... No, not junk mail, but most of us, get very few hand written letters anymore and it really stands out, when we do. Write them a personalized, thank you note.

To infuse your thank you with a dash of cleverness, try saying "mahalo" or perhaps "mahalo nui loa," which is the Hawaiian equivalent of thank you very much. Or Maybe "arigato" [ah-ree-gah-taw], which is thank you, in Japanese, merci or merci beaucoup to add a French flair or bring out your German side with a Danke [dahng-kuh]. Not a big deal, but it does add a bit of flair and makes the thank you more memorable, by speaking in a French accent and exaggerating your pronunciations.

The next section is not for many of you who sell to buyers at large companies, that can not receive gifts. Skip this part or dream of the day you could be a Realtor.... The world needs one more of those too.

Real estate agents and those in similar fields read on. The rest of you,

             don't be blue,

                        there's more for you.

Many Realtors, give a gift at closing. Often, it is always the same for every client, such as some sort of gift basket. Personally, I like the personal touches better. How about if you took a picture of your clients in front of their new home, while they are at the inspection or on your last visit, at the property

and then create "We're moving" postcards, that they can mail out to their friends. (maybe you include a, brought to you by Realtor Bob, note preprinted on the card)

I also like taking that same picture of your clients and creating, their own personalized postage stamp. How cool is that? Especially, if they didn't know you could do that. For $21.00 you can get 20 legal, first class stamps….. that have their photo on it. Go to : zazzle.com., photostamps.com or pictureitpostage.com. to create them. Why not be unique and give them something that they have never bought for themselves.

In our market, we have one of the largest Cutco salesmen in the country. He built his business around engraving Realtors names, on really nice knives and then the agents give them, as thank you gifts. I have heard that people really like them, because of their high quality and the Realtors get to keep their name front and center, every time they use them.

I have known agents that find a local artist, preferably one of your clients, that draws a penciled picture of their new home.

There is a website called reagentgifts.com that sells customized packing tape. Not a big thank you gift but pretty cool and has your name on it.

One of the things that makes a gift memorable, is if it is something that uniquely fits the recipient. What are their interests? If your client is a gardener, go buy a really cool ornamental shrub. Make sure it is something that stays small, so that they have many choices as to where to put it. If your client is known to enjoy a bottle of wine or a brewpub beer, you can buy cases of wine that have your own label on them, or many brewpubs sell growlers, that you can stick your personalized label on. Match their interest with your gift. If your client has kids, consider buying annual passes to the local zoo.

If your client is a big sports fan, consider a large

flag of their alma mater, that they can hang outside, on game day. You will find on the internet companies that make custom doormats, with the logo or design of your choice.

You get the idea. Skip the one size fits all, thank you gift and take a moment, to think of something that will have some staying power and let's them know that you made the effort, to get something they would find special.

Because, we are commission folks, it is OK to be a bit self-serving, so long as our heart is in the right place. Soooo, maybe you would send a thank you gift to someone's office. If you do, include helium filled balloons or flowers because they attract attention and the other people in the office, will ask them what the special occasion is. Since we want to make it easy for our clients to remember to give us referrals, why not attract attention from people that might say, I'm thinking of moving too. Perhaps you would include some of your business cards, with the gift and balloons.

My last thought on saying thank you is that whatever format you choose, is to make sure that you come from a place of sincerity. When in person, don't rush it. Stop and let them know that the comment is from your heart and not a knee jerk reaction thing, you say to everyone. If it is a gift, make it special. Daily, write down in a gratitude journal, what you are grateful for. Remember, saying thank you and being grateful, will have a huge positive impact on your life. It will bring you things you will be grateful for and want to say thank you for.

Hmmmm, what a tangled web we weave.

Bad Bob

Coach is the best and he told me once about shutting up. Actually, he says that a lot to me, but one time he was talking about how after I get an order to shut up because I keep talking so long my buyer might fall asleep or change his mind.

Old coach has many hidden messages in his words. This must be one of those because I know the advanced stage of this whole thank you deal must be to shut up and run after you get a commitment.

Coach likes to ease his students in to transitions. I bet this is one of those times where first he teaches us "thank you" and then after we master that, he will teach us to just say "thank you" with our eyes. Then we can combine thank you and shut up.

I believe from now when I get an order I will give them "the eye" and then never say another word as I pack up and leave.

Coach will be so proud.
Coach says I'm one of his best students.

We must believe
   that we are gifted
      for something, and
         that this thing, at
            whatever cost,
               must be attained.

Marie Curie

**I like being your friend
More than being your client...**

New Words=New Results

I propose, that the words we use, matter. It makes a huge difference in our results, because our clients react differently, to different words. Different words, different results, sometimes.

Many buying decisions are made from the heart. Often times, they are made from our emotional world. Some of you say I am wrong, because it is all price and delivery schedule. I get it, but the buyer wants certain people to win and is hesitant, towards others. It matters which group you are in. You get better information, chances to show your work etc., if you are in the favored group. They choose this group from whom they feel comfortable with. Maybe not consciously, but we all would rather work with folks we are comfortable with, than those we are not.

Words are part of our memory bank and their impact, won't be forgotten. We associate certain memories and feelings, with certain words. If someone uses words that have a negative connotation to you, you are uncomfortable. If they use the words that have pleasant memories and associations, then we are more comfortable.

The words that I use, are comfortable to me. The same is true for your clients. Use their words. Listen, and when appropriate, use the word that they would have used, in that sentence. We need to be aware to speak in words, that are in our clients normal vocabulary and thus, in their comfort zone. Those are the words that will make them feel warm and cozy and very comfortable.

Some buyers give purchase orders and some an order #.

Many of us "introduce" people, from time to time and are comfortable with the process, concept and the words. We are not as comfortable, "referring" someone, and have never been called upon to give one before. The last time they got a referral, they ended up half-naked in a cold room, with a proctologist.

People have warm feelings around the words "friends" and "family." If it fits your personality, refer to your client base as your "family of clients." Use the concept of, a closeness and a sharing, between all of you. Make a point of saying, "Welcome to the family" and hold reunions. When you introduce them to each other, do so as cousin Fred and Aunt Betty and make it fun. If you can't go that far, understand that those words, are better than client or customer, from the warm & fuzzy perspective.

People don't want to be "satisfied" with your service, they want to be "happy." Satisfaction either sounds like part of an overused, meaningless, guarantee or a Rolling Stones song, and we're not going there. People want to be happy.

If they say they are going to the beach this weekend, don't later acknowledge you love the shore. You love the beach.

If they show you their yard, do not love the lawn, love the yard.

If they say "How bout them Dawgs", don't next time say, "Man, the Huskies are doing great." The "Dawgs" are.

Maybe they have a spouse, but it might be their honey. Some people have a dog and some a puppy, pooch or best friend. Some folks have time to grab lunch but others would rather just grab a bite or get out of the office. I know people that exercise and some that workout, while even others go to the gym.

Don't over do it. Do not sound like you are mimicking them, because they will pick up on it. It is better to use their words a couple minutes after they did, than a couple seconds later. If it is an uncomfortable word for you, either don't use it or acknowledge out loud to the person "That is a funny word I never really use… Hmmm,(then repeat it) that's a pretty good word for that use, "Do not let them think you are being cute so go slow but just remember what word they would have used, in that sentence.

Most people like to "help" someone, if they can and if it is not a huge effort for them. Ask people to help. Tell them you are focusing on growing your business and you were wondering if they could "help" you out, with something?

We don't use the words "reticular activator" because those are our words, not the average person's, when we are asking for a referral. They are more likely to use the word "subconscious", which they are familiar with and a word, they have used before.

This is a great example of my point. We ask people for their business or for a referral, when they are in a "happy" place. If we use words like "reticular activator" to describe the process, their brain says "Say what? I don't know that word. Time for class, while Bobbo teaches me about that. Better get out of this emotional, I love Bob, happy place and go to my logical side." Then we ask them for..... OOPS.... That might have been a good time to use their comfort words and just get 'er done. We can be cool and impress people with our big words, another time.

Try to be a pro without sounding like a walking dictionary. Keep your words in the listener's language and comfort zone.

Seems like every time I open my mouth...

Bad Bob

Coach says that scripts do not start as a set of words. Rather, they are a several step process that we lead our clients through. Once we internalize those steps and the importance of doing them in the correct order, we can add the words that make sense. We create scripts with our words, that follow the specific steps of that particular script's process. It doesn't matter the words we use, so long as they take us through step one and transition into step two, etc.

We use a script, because it is nice to have words that come easily to us, that take us through the process we chose, as the most likely to succeed. We make them our words so that they flow comfortably to us and we can act natural.

Skip all that. Coach uses big words sometimes and to be honest, I have no idea what he's talking about, half the time. The key, is to use the words you are most comfortable with. I don't get the big deal about scripts. If those words are the words, that naturally fall out of my mouth, why do I need practice?
When the time comes, they will fall out again.

**When I let go of what I am,
  I become what I might be...**

LAO TZU

They're Everywhere….
I never noticed until I saw one, and now
I see them everywhere.
They started as a scab on my hand
and crept up to my face

Reticular Activator

The whole reticular activator conversation, is a very recent phenomena, but is widely accepted as an easy way to create a conversation about receiving referrals, from our clients. The conversation goes something like this:

Have you ever noticed how when you are pregnant, that all of a sudden, you are aware of pregnant ladies everywhere? Or bought a unique car that you really liked, but as soon as you drove it off the lot, you saw them everywhere? That is the part of the brain they call the reticular activator.

You then explain, how your business is the same way and now that they are buying this, they are going to be aware of people everywhere, wanting to buy the same thing. Does anybody come to mind that might be doing this, as we speak? If so, may I call them. If not, then I often find as soon as we leave or tomorrow at work, you will spot someone and think of me. Sometime, when we talk, may I ask you if you thought of anybody, after I left?

Whenever we are asking for business, we need our client to be in a "Happy Place." To do that, we need them to be in their comfort zone, so do not turn into the Little Professor and educate them about "Reticular Activator." We use examples that fit their lives. If they have young kids, we talk pregnancy. If they have a new van, we talk vans. If they have an ugly dog, well, you know. If they are regular folks, maybe we use the term "Subconscious" instead of "Reticular Activator."

What about me?

In addition, I would like to have you think about the reticular activator, from a different view. Don't just teach your client to look for opportunity, for you. Create a greater awareness in yourself, so that you recognize and then develop, more opportunities.

Understand the same thing, that we tell our clients will happen to them, happens to us. The reticular activator, is the foundation to many brainstorming techniques. The recommendation, is to start a separate file, where you capture all ideas about one specific BIG THING. Decide a worthy goal to achieve and come back and forth to it, constantly. Add notes and develop past ideas. Have a to do list and time projections. Enter crazy, creative ideas and thoughts on how to implement your idea.

The act of collecting all of the thoughts that our mind will throw at us, on a specific goal, sets our reticular activator, on fire. There is a huge compound effect, as the mind goes all sorts 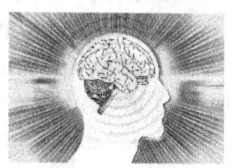 of directions and is given permission to create. The more times we come back to our notes and add to them, the greater awareness our "Reticular Activator" has. It will automatically spot possibilities all around the subject, you have chosen. When we hit these "on fire" stages, we need to carry something with us, to capture ideas immediately. Paper and pen, your phone, tablet etc. I have a small hand held recorder that takes one button to push and I am capturing that fabulous thought, before it is gone. I never miss a thought. I must have a dozen of those recorders and one is always close by.

This brainstorming style, is essential in developing:
--- a start-up business or project
--- career development
--- creating new marketing
--- choosing a new direction

Look at it often and continually capture, organize and analyze all ideas.

The key, is to do at least one of the "to do" items, or add to the notes, every day. Doesn't matter how small, but you continually collect and are constantly taking baby steps or bigger, in that direction daily.

The main concept of this chapter is to point out that the whole "Reticular Activator" deal is not just a closing tool. It is a closing tool, because it is real. If that is true, then we need to also develop it, within ourselves and not just ask our clients to do so.

We need to teach our clients to look for opportunity for us and we need to train ourselves to use it to its fullest advantage to direct our personal focus.

What we focus on, is what we find. Now you know why.

The Reticular Activator 201

Now that you get that part, let me back up and tell, as Paul would say, the rest of the story..... the reticular activator is actually a filter system.

There is too much data, that comes our direction and it would overwhelm our brains, if we had to categorize and remember, each item. We are not able to absorb it all. When we have brought a topic to the forefront of our lives, our reticular activator recognizes that topic, out of the flood of information, and allows that data to come to the forefront of our thoughts. If it is information that might be relevant to us, it allows it in. It tries to filter out the rest.... An attempt at sanity.

Focus on your Big Why and ideas will come from everywhere as your activator lets you see it all.

Bad Bob

This is nothing new. I have known about this activator concept since I was young. It first came up when I found that the belly button occasionally held some edible lint and then graduated to a higher scale when I discovered that if I used my fingernails to scrape off that gunk on my teeth, I would never get cavities.

The doctor referred to it as obsessive compulsive something, with a side order of some diaper changing issues. He says, sometimes if we fixate on one thing, that becomes all that we can think about. I think that was the obsessive part but now we call it "reticular activator." I am here to tell you, it is true. If you really focus on one thing, like cleaning your teeth, you can really get a lot done. I would get in the zone and get lost with my hands working every spot between each tooth for hours.

You do have to be a little careful though, as to what you focus on.

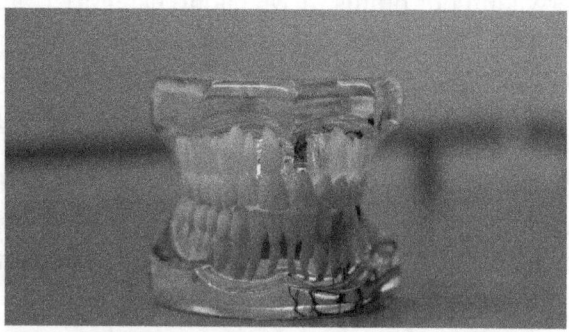

Is it proper, to beat a client?

Just thought I should check, mate

Chapter Seventeen

Less is the New More

With a title like, "Less is the New More, " I bet you are thinking I am going to talk about living the simple life, about having a garage sale and de-cluttering your surroundings and thus your mind. You are assuming, I am gong to try and impart wisdom, about growing your own organic food and gathering Puka Shells or some other such nonsense. You will be sorely disappointed and equally disappointing is the fact that my target audience, skipped this chapter because of the title….

Noooooo, I'm a business coach, not the Dalai Lama. I'd like to talk about, less being the new more, as a daily business model, to kick butt and have a great career.

Let's specifically address the, "To Do" list. In order to do that, let's look at the "List" historically speaking. When I kicked into the sales thing, it was 1975 and we were all taught to keep a running "To Do" list, on a legal sized yellow pad and use black ink. I promise. It was very effective, because we could add new things at the bottom of the page, or if that was full, just continue on the next page. It was genius, eh? We would cross off those we accomplished, kept adding all the new great ideas as they came to us and they were all on one pad we could carry around. In 1975 terms, we're talking, Boomshackalacka….

There has been some evolution, as the compute came along. We are now able to input our never ending "To Do," list electronically. But to this day, that mindset persists, among many. You have a monster long list of things, you could and perhaps should do. I know, many of us are so sophisticated as to have them segmented into "A", "B" and even that infamous "C" category. That way we really focus on those A's and B's first.

The problem comes, when our lists are long enough, that all of the A's, do not get done in one day. They carry over because in the Big Picture, they are an A, even if not one that I can do, today. We are of a mindset, that all of these A's are important and so are the B's, so I need to get as many of them done as possible. We do some of the A's, a few of the B's and accidentally, got a couple C's done.

When we look at our day and plan out our activities, we are better to narrow down our, "To DO" list to a "To DO Today," list which is drastically shorter. Sure we have our to do's, captured somewhere and we work off of that, but it gives a false sense of accomplishment, if we just scratch a few of those off everyday. The question is, if you had picked 1-3 "Absolutely, Most Valuable To Your Long Term Career, I Am a Stud if I Do These" list and really committed to doing them...... how much better off would you be next year? For you see, the goal is not to have a good year, the goal is to have a great life.

This list of 1-3 items does not include:

Call John and confirm order shipped
Figure bid for "X Company"
Workout
Do my expense report

The "To Do Today" list is short and forward thinking. It evolves around making sure we don't get wrapped up, in returning urgent phone calls, and that each day, we make some progress toward our bigger goals. It might include:

Write a chapter for my book
Check into joining Rotary
Call boss to meet for lunch
Prep my lunch agenda for boss
Develop a new niche
Run an ad for an assistant
Hold a board meeting with yourself
Signup for online class
Call so-and-so and pick his brain
Find a mentor
Ask X for a referral to Y
Find a piece of business for someone else

I recommend that you print out your list. I know, pretty darned old school, now don't you know, eh? But it has value, to be able to hold it in your hands and touch it. You are using one more sense and that helps commitment. It is also much more dramatic for my pea brain, to manually cross off something, with a pen. When I feel like a rebel…. I use blue ink or dare I say, red?

Ask yourself a question, "Have you ever once in your career, completed a "To DO" list?" Of course not. They really aren't intended, to actually be, accomplished. They are designed to chip away at. So we do, and we feel really good about ourselves at the end of the day. Wow, I crossed off 7 A's and a bunch of B's.

When we teach ourselves, even more, condition ourselves really, that we never have to, or are ever expected to, complete the "A" list, the most important things, we personally decided we should do, it allows us to assume failure. By having an ad infinitum… to infinity and beyond, "To Do" list, we take away all of our personal accountability. At the end of the day or the week, we can feel great that we crossed off so many things and of course, I never expected to "DO," the things on my, "TO DO" list. Well, I mean sure, I kinda, sorta hope I do all of them over time, unless I downgrade them to a "B" later, but I need to keep these as an "A on my list…

If the distinction is too vague, try this. Keep your same lists. In addition add one "A+" list that is tiny and only addresses:

How do I get a promotion?

Steps towards starting my own business.

Patenting that good idea.

Most important to develop my career.

When the purpose of this "Tiny List," is to keep our ship on track, for the long course, we accept that we can't do a monster thing everyday, to that end. Many of the most important, "To DO Today"

Full Steam Ahead

items, are incredibly small. They aren't necessarily the most exciting or dramatic event of the day. They just make sure that we don't ever spend a day, without doing one or more things, that are directed to our bigger goal and not just the goal of this week or year.

More examples of a Monster item on your "To Do Today" list might be:

Google resume writing
Take a free online personality profile test
Read one Chapter of…
Call Uncle Fred to meet 4 lunch. Talk…
Practice one closing script
One hour on your online class
Call the senior salesperson and meet for lunch
Research the company you wish you were at

When my list is long, there is no way to monitor if I met my commitments. The list becomes meaningless, just a bunch of things, some of which I'll do and some of which I won't.

This really leads us to the "Urgent" vs. "Important" question. I get it that calling back your best customer, is urgent and must be done, or you won't be here in a year…. Many things that are very urgent and yes, important kinda, sorta, are not really Big Picture items, that would make the list of, most important things to affect my career next year.

Don't lose track of the infinite number of baby steps required, to make the Big Leap. We do what is urgent, so that we can eat and survive. If we don't continually keep our eye looking down the road and commit to some effort daily that helps us on that path, it is easy to get lost. Building the habit of some small step daily, keeps us focused and

Can't see the finish line?

Start anyway…

great things happen when we focus.

One of the biggest benefits, of learning to check off every single thing on your to do list, is that it builds integrity. As you complete everything that you said you would, you teach yourself, to do everything that you tell yourself, you will do. Integrity to one's self is rare, because it is so easy to convince ourselves. We know our favorite excuses.

Imagine the mental shift. At the end of the day, instead of, "Had a great day and did a bunch of things" you can truly acknowledge that you did everything you committed to yourself to do, because they were the most important things for you, to keep on track for a great life. No matter what your current struggles are, if you can look in the mirror every night, and know you have taken the steps today, to get you to a GREAT LIFE, you can sleep well.

Less is the New More.

Bad Bob

Coach is great. He gets it. I see some of these salespeople putting in long hours. They are at the office early, planning their day and doing less valuable tasks. Some of these idiots, study at night and spend all day chasing, chasing, chasing prospects.

Aye Yi Yi, who would do that? Only the lost and confused, perhaps those without a business coach, would be so unfocused.. Me, I've learned to do less, a lot less than the others. I just focus in on one thing everyday, that is important, and I get 'er done. Because I know when you plan your schedule, you always put in your time-off first, some days the only thing I get done, is taking time off. Cool.

Thanks coach.

Your time is limited,

so don't waste it living someone else's life.

Steve Jobs

**I don't wanna ask any questions,
						if I have to answer them.**

2 most Important Questions 2 Improve your Business

There are a million good ideas that, if we implemented into our lives, would have a positive impact. They go from a small, non-event thing, to a major commitment and lifestyle change. In this section, let's simplify things and look at two sentences, if asked and answered honestly, could be as impactful to your lives, as any major commitment.

Because I am a big fan of under promise and over deliver, let me say that, these two questions can take you from struggling, to a monster salesperson….. or #1 to untouchable King…and that is an under promise…..

Don't change anything else in your life. Just respond to these two questions. They not only will change your career, but have a short term, immediate impact, on your business as well….. er… uh… if you choose to ACT on the new information that is. Hmmmm, maybe I should do a chapter on how thoughts are not enough. It still takes action and commitment…. Nah... No one would want to read about that.

Question #1

What should I do more of, which would have the biggest impact, on my business?

Because it has the highest value
Because you are the best at it
Most Important long-range activity
Most Urgent short term for income
New niche development
Because you are the only one to do it
Productive activity that I avoid
Productive thing I did when I was new

Question #2
What should I do less of, that would have the greatest positive impact, on my business or life?

Takes a lot of my time
Drains my energy
Activity or client that wastes my time
Easily replace me. "Anyone can do it"
    activities
Low dollar return for the activity
Someone else is better. Pay them or learn it.
Someone less expensive than me, can do it.
An addiction that holds me back
A bad influence: person or place

Folks, this is easy.
You don't have to do this everyday, but this is not one and done. Incorporate the concept into your business model, to make major decisions and small corrections. I suggest you make it part of your weekly Board Meeting, with yourself. Think Big Picture. If you choose to be headed to the ideal career, what one thing do you need to start doing and what one thing do you need to stop doing, to keep on track or to adjust to, "on track."

Remember, the question was, the one thing, that would have the greatest impact. Greatest impact. Do not cheat and add or subtract something that is a good idea, and a lot easier to do, but that is not the one biggest thing that would have the greatest impact… unless #2 or #3, is all you can handle now, then do that.

This does not alone, guarantee monster businesses, but should give you the biggest bang for the buck and immediate results. Really, sit down and without all the data, that many great, long-term plans have attached to them, just decide what will give you an immediate increase in performance or results (both long and short term goals) Do it this week.

The key is to commit, to doing whatever those two things are. You probably already know that you could be more successful if you…… Decide that it is now, so obvious, that you really should do it. Choose integrity to yourself.

As everyone's favorite, Forrest, would say "And that's all I have to say about that."
Give m a BOOYAH for simple and a
BOOMSHACKALACKA for relevant.

Good Point.
If you should do it, do it.

Bad Bob

Coach says that you have to take mentoring advice and adapt it to your own style. The same with all success models. Take the best ideas and re-work them just enough, that you can feel comfortable, owning that model.

That must apply to the whole "2 questions" deal. Coach has the right idea, but I'm not sure those are the right 2 questions for me. They might work for him, but the title was the 2 "GREATEST" questions and so I have searched my brain and decided what works for me.

When I look at what I should do more of, it is obvious. In order to have a clear mind and be rested and ready to go, I need way more vacation. Way more.

If I ask myself what should be removed from my life, I first had to analyze what it is that I hate. When I do it, I feel worse than if I hadn't… and yet I keep doing it over and over. Coach thinks we should reduce the frequency of doing those wrong things. I say coach is a wimp and if it is not good, we should eliminate it entirely, not just reduce it.

Me, I hate alarm clocks and when that darn thing goes off, it starts my day, in a terrible way. If I want to be my best, I need to guard against things, that throw me into a bad mood. From now, I choose to wake up naturally, as God intended. Slowly and when the mind and body, are fully refreshed. That way, I will be much more productive, with the few hours that I am awake.

**All of Coach's advice
has given me great direction.**

Empty Chairs???

Better than a Super Bowl ad…

Chapter Nineteen

BIG GROUPS
BIG BUCKS

I would like to talk about something, that is seldom done by salespeople or most companies, but something that uses your time very efficiently. This idea sets you apart, as a unique and value adding person, that creates synergy by bringing together your clients under one roof, and is just down right cool.

That is, putting on large, group meetings, of interest. If you currently, never bring together any clients, then a group of 2 is big, as well. I'm not talking about trade shows or gatherings, you call education, but are really meant as demo time, for some manufacturer or product.

What if you found reasons, to create gatherings that people would find interesting, informative and enhance your image.

Why

Build deeper relationships in a relaxed setting
Synergy of your clients talking together about you
Show charisma, when stand up and briefly speak
Look like a leader, if you are in control of the setting

One great idea, is to put on a candidates night. Every election season, the candidates are desperately looking for ways to get in front of voters, and many voters welcome a chance to see their choices live, and ask them questions. Call a couple candidates to pick a date.If one is available, then they all will be, because they travel the same circuit and are busy the same nights. If their competitor is going to be there, trust me, they will try very hard to be available.

Invite your entire database. If that does not fill a room, let the paper know and they will publicize it. Have people write down questions they would like asked, of particular candidates or positions. In order to have their question asked, they must include their name. which allows you the chance to call them back and thank them, for their involvement. Let each candidate speak for 3-5 minutes. Have someone be the timer, whom raises a card, when time is up. After they have spoken, have a Q & A period, where you either read the questions or you let people come up, and ask their question.

Don't turn it into a big marketing campaign for you. The goal is to add value to your folks and to increase your presence, in the community, without looking too obvious about it. I have done this and the response was huge.

Perhaps at the beginning of tax season, give a free tax tips seminar. You will easily be able to find an accountant, that would like the publicity and clients that are appreciative to listen. Make sure the accountant you choose, has some speaking skills, he/she is accountant, after all.

The whole gluten free thing, has become a major topic and many people are still learning, about it. Find a couple of experts, that can give research data and recipes and lifestyle tips. The people that do come, will be very appreciative. Find a way to capture the names of who came and follow up to see if there is any more info on the topic, you can gather.

Consider Investment Advice night, where you have a financial advisor, a stockbroker, an accountant and someone who can talk about the local real estate opportunities. Give each a few minutes to talk and have a Q & A period.

When a new bridge or freeway ramp is going in, invite the local politicians or government employee that knows about it, as well as the construction company foreman and educate people, about the topic.

Find a location where you can have a large group of football fans come together. When the Super Bowl or the local college team, has a big game, be party central and create a monster, fun party. (no alcohol unless you hold it at a bar where someone else has the liability) Get a table and bring together a few clients, that share the same passion for the home team, at the sports bar.

In the spring you could easily find a nursery owner, that would come and bring a couple experts with him, to speak about gardening tips.

People go nuts trying to help their kids get an advantage, in the sport of their choice. Why not gather together a couple coaches and put on a free kids soccer, basketball or whatever clinic. You could help out or you could mingle with parents, while it went on.

Many towns have a local parade that you can participate in, for free. Find a flat bed truck and decorate it up a bit. Invite your clients' kids to ride on it and give them bags of candy to throw.

As fishing season approaches, hold a fly casting or???? seminar, for the fisherman.

Our company, has rented out a whole theater for our clients, thrown a Back to School Carnival, where all kids got free school supplies and A Christmas Craft Fair, where they made free crafts with help from elves and a pic with the Real Santa. Really, it might be. This guy was great.

Our clients look forward to our annual events.

When you have free , "concerts in the park," in your area, go down early and set up 20 or 50 chairs, that you have reserved for your clients. You can buy lawn chairs for about $6.00. You could have 50 of them for $300. In my area, they hold a summer series and you could use those same chairs, 8 or 9 times. For a few bucks you

could bring together people, that you'd like to get to know better, 8 or 9 times. Incredible value for the money, and what a relaxed way to build relationships.

There are possibilities of cooking tips for vegetarians, study or behavioral tips for parents with youngsters, college prep classes and on and on. Whatever would be an interesting topic, for some segment of your clients and prospects, works. It also works well, when you have one on a topic, that you are passionate about, but not necessary.

Bad Bob

Coach says, if I can figure out this Big Group thing, it will make me more efficient with my time. I think I might be a bit nervous standing up in front of a Big Crowd and speaking, unless it was something I knew a lot about or was very passionate about.

Here's what I'm thinking.
I could rent a bus and give my best prospects all a ride to the State College game about 2 hours away. I'd slip Everclear into the punch and have an instant Big Party Bus…. They would never forget me. That's something I know I'm good at, plus after several of those punch drinks, I love to talk and tell jokes in front of a Big Crowd. I might go ahead and spend a bit of that big payoff, that is coming. Maybe I could buy everybody on the party bus, a State College jacket, and then after the game, let them know that they can keep it, if they give me an order. If not, please wash it and return it to my office, before next week's big game.

Hey Mister, where you headed???

Chapter Twenty

Commute
Your Way to Success

Guess what I am going to talk about.

If you added up the minutes of your life, that you spent in a car alone, and really internalized those numbers, I believe many would use that time, differently. I suggest that you take a week and have a journal in the car. Track the # of hours you spend driving around, while no one else is in the car.

Let me help: The average salesperson spends 10 hours (Minimum) per week, which would include travel back and forth to your office or starting point, as well as any driving needed, to get to appointments. We work 48 weeks per year and in our average sales career of 25 years, we spend 12,000 hours listening to traffic updates and commercials, with a dash of whatever. 12,000 hours. If we count a workday, as 9 hours, that equals 1,333 complete work days, filled with nonsense poopy pants stuff.

That's the math. If we used that time or most of that time, to build our business, develop our skills or lift our spirits, it would have to have a positive effect, right?

When we talk about doing the little things to be successful, this is the type of thing we are referring to. Not some huge, life changing commitment, that is hard to keep. A little thing. Just use most, of that wasted windshield time, and become better. Here are some starting points to consider:

Build Your Business

--- Make 2 extra phone calls in to your database everyday. Have a list in the car or on your phone, of who those choices are, so it is always with you. Do it legally.

--- Turn off the radio and use a recording device, to brainstorm about good ideas for your business. This really works well if you do it often, because the brain catches on that we are going to brainstorm now, and is ready. If you choose this, set aside a time, that you retrieve those messages and capture those ideas.

Develop Your Skills

--- This is a perfect time to practice your scripts. If you're headed to an appointment, practice one, that you might use at that appointment. Have them written down, so you can glance over and remember the words. Practice inflection and casual effects, such as laughing, pausing, smiling, nodding, turning your head to listen etc.
--- Is there a continuing education course you could take, that is on C.D. or online, and that you could listen to while driving?

Lift Your Spirits

--- If we read ten pages a day, of a good business oriented book or something of the self-help nature, we'd read more than a dozen good books per year. You can't possibly tell me, that there is not some benefit, from that. Most of us don't read that much once we get home.

Do it in the car, with a C.D. The library will have some good ones you may borrow. Ask your colleagues if they have something they bought at a seminar or that they like, and borrow them. You may also choose to invest in your own library.
--- First thing I would do, is print out my affirmations and have them with me, in the car. As you drive into work in the morning, read them and contemplate each one, after you read it. I think it will be safe if you set them down next to you and glance over to remind yourself of one, and then ponder it for a few blocks, as you drive to the office. What a fabulous way to start your day. Just that one thing, could make a huge difference in your attitude, as you arrive to work, ready to go.

We are always saying, how there aren't enough hours in the day. Well, here is a way to capture some of them and to do something positive, for your business. Do not let this turn into passive listening. Really listen and ask yourself the personal questions, that are needed to grow. Make sure you get in the habit of controlling the message, by pausing and rewinding the audio as needed, to internalize the message.

Going my way?
I commute, wisely.

Bad Bob

This coach deal, is working out great. He says to use my commuting time, wisely. He says to develop a strategy, as to how I best use this time. He says, he invented this idea, the guy is brilliant.

Here is my strategy…. Hmmm, maybe I should be a coach….

Way to work. I need to arrive ready to go, so I commit to drinking a couple of Red Bulls and continually slap myself in the face. Some days I will start with the slapping and some days, they will be the big finish, just before I get to my office.

Drive to an appointment. I will always drive through Starbucks and get a Grande Espresso, before every appointment. I commit to chugging it, if the meeting is close to my office. I will always listen to sports in the car so that I will have something to talk about during the appointment. I will always lead with a sports comment, while it is still fresh in my mind.

Drive back to office: Everyday I will practice my scripts after an appointment. I will put emphasis on different syllables in the phrase "How bout Dem Huskers?" until it flows naturally for me.

Drive Home: I commit to start drinking on the way home, so I can get a jump on the evening's activities. That should allow my buzz to kick in during "Jeopardy" which will be a serious upgrade over not feeling until the NCIS re-runs.

Sometimes I am amazed, that I am only a couple of chromosomes upstream, from this Bad Bob guy.

There's BIG BUCKS
In Quilts

Chapter Twenty One

Segmentation
(The Wave of the Future)

…… and by "Wave of the Future", I mean that if you do not integrate segmentation into your business relationship development, wave good bye to your future.

We build, nurture and then harvest, from our database. In professions like stockbrokers, Realtors, lenders, insurance, accountants, (and now even medical doctors with the new concierge style of practice) etc., we purposely choose who we would like to work with, over the years. We target them and develop them, for our whole career. We just need to identify them, let them know that we own them & that they will hear from us forever. (pronounced very slowly…foooooooreeeeeevvvverrrrrrrrr)

They now, are our database, CRM or book of business, as you choose.

When we are lucky, or perhaps when we are wise, the same concept applies to corporate type salespeople. In order to win the race (as in rat), you need help. Help from people above you, your peers who like you, the inside support group, your competitors, (Who might hire you someday) and the manufacturers or suppliers, upstream from your company. You have a database of people that you will run across your whole career. The key is to identify them and nurture them.

In other places, I talk about identifying, building and harvesting. That is all the easy part. The hardest for most of us, is to "Nurture." I will sound sexist here, but you all know the mature, female, successful Realtor-type, that knows everybody, and is always in an animated conversation with somebody. She loves people and remembers their dog's name and their aunt Susie in Minnesota, now don't you know, eh and starts up a conversation everywhere. She doesn't even prospect. She goes to the dog park with her mangy little terrier and comes away with a listing, from someone, she just met. Same, in the corporate world. some funny guy, has something to easily to say, to everyone.

That does not describe me. When I started developing my future clients, into a database, I would call to keep in touch and nurture them. The conversation usually went something like this:

Bob: Dial…dial…. Ring……..
Potential A+ client for life prospect: Hello
Bob: Hello John, this is Bob Bloom
Potential A+ client for life prospect: Well hi Bob, great to hear from you. How are you?
Bob: Fabulous, and how are you and Jill doing?
Potential A+ client for life prospect: Both real good, thanks.
Bob: Great, and how are the kids doing?
Potential A+ client for life prospect: Good, good, Bob…..
Bob: Good… good….
Bob: So good, glad to hear you guys are good. How's work going?
Potential A+ client for life prospect: Good, real good………..
Bob: Oh, good.
Potential A+ client for life prospect: …. and so, how are your kids?
Bob: Good. Yeah, they are both doing good…
Bob: Thanks for asking.
Potential A+ client for life prospect: Uhm, so uh….
Bob: I didn't want to take a lot of your time just glad you are good.
Potential A+ client for life prospect: Good, good..
Bob: Well it was good to talk to you,…. Oh by the way, do you happen to know anybody that is thinking of moving?
Potential A+ client for life prospect: Boy, nobody comes to mind at the moment.
Bob: Well if you ever think of anybody, would you call me?
Potential A+ client for life prospect: Absolutely. That would be good.
Bob: Good, good. Thank you.
Potential A+ client for life prospect: Good enough. Bye Bob.

Potential A+ client for life prospect: Hmmmmmm...
Potential A+ client for life prospect's wife: Who was that
      honey?

Potential A+ client for life prospect: Realtor Bob.
Potential A+ client for life prospect's wife: Great. I love that
      guy. What did he want.
Potential A+ client for life prospect: I'm not sure. It was really
weird. I guess he was just asking for a referral or
      something. It wasn't a very good conversation.

Two Months Later

Bob: Dial....Dial.....Ring....
Potential A+ client for life prospect: Oh no......

      Ring....Ring....Ring.....

Potential A+ client for life prospect's wife: Honey, if you are
      busy, do you want me to get that?
Potential A+ client for life prospect:

NOOOOOOOO.
IT'S BAAAHHHHHHBBBB!!!

   The problem for many database developers, is that it is way
too awkward, to call people for years, to nurture them. For me, it
was impossible to continually call someone, when I had no purpose
in calling.
   Yes, we can mail them monthly, which works for some %,
but another %, needs the call. I don't have to pretend, that I
invented the fact, that an in-person visit, has greater effect, than a
newsletter. Right after the in-person in value, is a phone call and a
real conversation.
   I just can't do it. I can not comfortably call, and have a
warm and endearing conversation, unless I have a purpose to

call. I knew that was a huge weakness for me, and I had to overcome it. You can imagine, how well that worked. A nervous, uncomfortable, sales guy, that is not great at small talk, putting extra pressure on himself, to be witty and clever. I won't type out that conversation for you, but believe me, it was much shorter.

The key to me having a chance, to have "Potential A+ Client for life prospect," look forward to hearing from me when I called, was if I had something to say. Hmmmmmmmm. Wow, something like a purpose for the conversation that gave me direction.

My only hope was to segment my database. I just had to categorize them into segments that I can identify and call up as needed. WWDD. What Would Dale Do? Good old Dale Carnegie, might have said, that it would be very

I own this turf...

interesting to my clients, if I called and talked to them, about what they think, is very interesting. (....AHA....) The question became: What do they think is interesting? I was clueless. I was clueless, because I had not yet segmented my database. Now it is easy.

In my CRM (database system), I have searchable categories such as gardener, Oregon Duck fan, music or wine lover, fisherman or hunter, loves to cook, Christian, atheist, loves dogs, golfer, has kids, sports nut, runner, has a boat, but that is a different purpose...connection to Oklahoma, connection to Colorado, big basketball fan etc.

I say " Hi Fred this is Bob Bloom. I was thinking of you today and just had to call, I heard on the radio, the annual yard and garden show is this weekend and it made me think of you and your incredibly beautiful yard. Are you going to the show?'

.....or I say " Hey Fred, I was thinking about you today and just had to call, how bout them Ducks, eh. Big game this weekend"

....or I say "I was thinking of you today and just had to call. March Madness starts tomorrow and I am clueless. I know you probably already have all the winners picked and maybe you could give me some insight, before I look stupid and fill out my bracket."

....Or I say "I was thinking of you today and just had to call. Do I remember that you were from Oklahoma? And she will say yes and I will say, I was concerned when I heard about the tornadoes. It looked really bad. Do you have any family that was affected?"

.....or "Hey I know you love to go shoot up those elk, are you going this weekend?"

....or "I was thinking of you today because I heard they are having a dog show, out at the coliseum and I know how much you love your pooches."

....or "I just had to call. I saw there is a seminar on gluten free cooking and I thought of you."

....or "Oh my gosh Joe, I saw they have candidates night at the school auditorium and I know you love politics."

....or "Jill, I hope it is OK to call, I saw they are looking for cooks to bring their best sample for a chili cook-off, and when I think of great cooks, girl you are it. That meal you made, me is still in my top 2 all-time favorites. I can't imagine what you could do with chili."

....or "I was thinking of you when I saw the season schedule came out, for the free concert in the park, series. Have you seen it or can I email you a copy?"

....or "I know you are new in town. I just thought of you when I was talking with a friend, about the monthly art crawl downtown. It is a nice way to get to know downtown and meet some people. Have you heard about that yet?"

....or "Jane, I had to call. I heard on the radio about the shooting at XYZ University. Doesn't your daughter go there?"

....or "Mary, I was thinking of you today and I just had

**Never Miss
Veteran's Day**

to call. I know your son's over in the Middle East. today, on Veteran's Day. I wanted to call and see how he is doing. Thank them for their contribution. Let them know you appreciate them and their son, and share with them, the most meaningful conversation, they could have in life. How is their child, whom is in harm's way, doing? They are proud and scared. They will remember that you care.

Not just their kids. If someone has sacrificed for our country, they will love to be acknowledged, on their day. Ask them some light details about their experience. Next time you will know where they served. Build your database of data.

When you get segmented, never again, miss thanking the past and current veterans. That, is an easy one.

When I hang up, they are glad that I called. We have further cemented our relationship and they like me, even more. We had a nice short conversation, about something they want to talk about. Sometimes I ask for a lead and sometimes I don't, but if I do, they know, that is not why I called.

Next time I call, they answer the phone " BOB, HOW ARE YOU......and are excited to hear from me.

So, how do we do this?

The most important step is, to use a CRM system that allows you to develop your own categories. It has to have the ability for you to develop" unlimited" categories (or segments I call them) of your own.

There is no software currently available, that has every category, that you need. When you run across someone that graduated from the University of Nebraska or is a quilter, you need to be able to create that category. Then we learn to keep our eyes open for signs and ask pointed questions, that we keep track of the answers.

If we see they have pictures of grandkids, we can easily remember that, when we see an article on how to speak to kids about drugs.

If they have a plant on their desk, I categorize them and then know whom to call, when the yard and garden show comes to town.

If I see a Christian symbol, I am not going to send a "Happy Holidays" card in December. I am going to send a "Merry Christmas" card, because that is the segment.

I mention quilter. I recently heard on the radio about the "Quilters Show." I couldn't remember if I had any, but I pulled up "quilter," and found that I apparently, have 2 clients, that are into the whole quilting thing. I called and said " I was thinking of you today…." I'm telling you, they loved me. Two for two, thanked me. One said, that she would try and get me a referral sometime soon, if she could. I believe they both went to the event.

It is not enough to put that information into the remarks section of your database. You need to have software that allows you to create unlimited search fields. The data does you no good, unless you can search for all of those, that fit into a category, with one button. The goal is to have a database of clients and future clients, that is way too big, to remember all your quilters.

I don't care what you use, but most CRM software has a pretty small limit on the number of search categories, that you can create. You need a lot.

I know ACT allows you to search by any word, so
that, works. I have used them. I currently use Realty Juggler
and pay $99./year. It does not have the most bells and
whistles, which I don't care about, but it lets me build
unlimited search fields.

This has no value if you don't train yourself, to look for
the things that would be fun or interesting to somebody. Perhaps
not you, but apparently, somebody. Pay attention to the radio ads
for events. Make a habit of checking the entertainment section in
the newspaper and local entertainment blogs, to find reasons to
call.

Once again, this definitely applies to the corporate types, as well
us independents. If you know your boss or a client, was a veteran,
call them. If your customer service rep, that helps you so much,
has pictures of her dog at work, take note. Before an appointment
or going to a trade show, stop and look up the profiles of the
people that you will bump into. Make notes of what is interesting
to different business contacts, that will be at the show, and stick
them in your pocket. Review your notes privately as needed. It
will blow them away, when you remember the little details,
which are the biggest details, to them in their life. It is what they
find interesting and they will love you for it.

Segment your database and your clients will love you.
They will look forward to hearing from you, instead of using
caller ID, to screen you. There is much talk about relationship
selling. In order to build a relationship, you need to go deep.
Find what they find interesting and figure out how to develop
that.

Bad Bob

This concept was a little overwhelming for me, at 1ˢᵗ .
To create unlimited searchable categories, or segments, would
take a long time. I couldn't even think of eight, right off.

Coach said that if it was too much to comprehend, just
start with all of my past and current clients, my prospects and
all of my friends and family, in the area.

That made it a lot easier to understand. I finally
understood that whole, long and boring, elephant eating
story coach told. I would break it down and over the first year
of my career, eat an ear. I love elephant ears.

Since I didn't know anyone that fit into any of those
categories, it was much more manageable of a task. I can
honestly tell coach, that I am completely segmented with all
my friends and family, that still talks to me. He will be so proud.

I like zombie stuff. Maybe year two, I will focus on
developing, that segment.

Now that, I could be passionate about! Zombie specialist…

Daily goals

Become a balancing act, between responsiveness and short sightedness.

Weekly Goals

Thought I would introduce you to a topic, that you most likely have never heard anything about... Goal setting. O.K., some of you may have some thoughts on that. Here is one of mine.

There is much attention given, to the topic of establishing and meeting daily goals. The whole "time blocking" and daily commitments to your, "get 'er done" list. Best laid plans.....For many of us, things beyond our control, pop up and need our immediate attention. Yes, we need to learn to limit or delegate those, but still, it happens. We have no chance of doing all of the things, we committed to do, today.

When that does happen, you are just another lousy, stinking failure. You made a commitment 9 hours ago and couldn't even keep your word, to yourself, for one day. Loser!   Really. If we have a specific, "To Do Today" list, that we created with much thought and commitment, and then we don't do it, our brain remembers. It remembers that you made a commitment and didn't meet it, but that's O.K. cuz...... it happens. No big deal.

It is a huge deal. If we train ourselves to make a commitment to ourself, and it is alright to break it, we lower our personal integrity. We get used to not doing, what we said we would. Our subconscious knows, that we don't have to do all that stuff, just make a good list and try. When we have many things on our "To Do Today" list, we fail more often.

I love the "Weekly To Do" list, as well as a shorter, daily commitment list. There are always things, that need to get done today, but many of our activities are meant to build our business and just need to get done over and over, every week.

I believe we lose integrity to ourself, and our word becomes meaningless, if not kept. You can't fake it with your own mind. You either did what you committed to do, or not.

So what should our weekly goals be? They should always be "activity" goals, and never sales goals. We can not control when we get a sale or when we get the signed paperwork. Sometimes we will have huge months and sometimes, it seems like nothing is coming together. If our goal is to have 4 sales and we have 2, then we are a failure and the emotional roller coaster rolls on. We should not set ourselves up for failure, by having goals that we can not control. The only thing we can control for sure, is what we do. Our activities.

Internalize that for a second. If at the end of the week, your honey asks, "How was your week?" the answer is "Fabulous," even though you didn't make one sale. When we, and more importantly, those around us, think we judge ourselves by short-term results, meaning sales, it is crippling. If it is about sales, then my week sucked and my mother-in-law was right. I'm a loser. Zero sales all week. Back to flippin' burgers.

But as we teach ourselves and our support system, that we are building a Monster Career, and am committed to do those activities that get me there, every week....

Boomshackalacka, Baby. I had a fabulous week, and met all my goals. I am on my way. Are you horny?

I believe this is important. The first time, your spouse or dad, asks how was week, did you sell anything, we need to set the ground rules and explain what we are doing. We explain what activities are important to us to build a career. Then in the future dad will ask "Did you get your five new prospects this week, boy?" Our weekly goals, should be to do those things that assure, we will always get more than our share. That is something we have complete control over.

Those weekly activities would include things like:

Prospecting: We all need to continue to prospect, whether that is for new clients, or new sales out of our existing client base. I used to commit to adding 5 people to my database every week, even if they were not buyers, currently. Many would set prospecting goals, as a number of phone calls/contacts or hours spent per week.

Current Business: Some of us only have a few clients at a time, or we only have a few "A+" clients, that deserve regular attention. I commit to having at least one contact with each of those, every week. Sometimes, there is nothing to talk about and so we don't have a single communication all week, with our most important clients. Not a good idea. If by Friday, you have not had a purpose to touch in, find one or call and say "nothing to say this week, but I wanted to see if you need anything from me, before the week is over?"

Many of us have clients, that we seldom speak to. They may be a solid core, of our business, but it flows smoothly and there is no real purpose to be touching in often. Some of these end up slipping into the "never talk to" category. Each week, it is not urgent and you are busy. I suggest, you create a list of them and call X number, per week. Just a few, but be consistent. It will save you business, that eventually will be vulnerable, and will force you to ask if there is any other area, where you might be of help.

Self Improvement: Many of the top performers, practice their scripts weekly. They change and adapt them, but even after years of selling, they keep sharp, with weekly practice. For some of us, we could earn designations within our field, that would enhance our image and knowledge, by taking some further education.

This also, is where you commit to reading X # of chapters, in a self-improvement type book.

Practice

Your Future: Some of you have dreams of being something else, or

In the Mirror

starting something new, someday. Never let a week go by, that you don't do something, to that end.

Board Meeting: I talk about this elsewhere, but this is always on my weekly list. I put my feet up and spend some uninterrupted time, thinking Big Picture thoughts, about my business.

Your Health: It is hard to get to the gym some days, but there is no excuse why we can't make it, X times per week. I include meditation and my affirmations, in my health section and commit to X times per week. I would include any spiritual development, in this category.

Your Personal Life: Radical thought, but it takes more than work, to be fulfilled. Make sure a week never slips by, that you let your loved ones be ignored. Think of ways to make the family time you have, be special.

Don't ignore the fact that you need to be you and express yourself, in a hobby or activity, that is uniquely you.

Referrals: Many of us get great value, from receiving referrals. Many of us, seldom ask for one. Make it a weekly habit, to at least ask for a referral, X# of times.

Other: Many experts believe, you should write hand written thank you notes, for a bigger impact. You might commit, to writing 5 per week.

If you have figured out the value of a gratitude journal, write your commitment here.

Got the idea? Decide which activities are critical, if you are going to have a great year, as well as a great career, and track them. I actually print this list out and look at it, throughout the day. I literally put a check in each box, as I do one of the items and it really keeps me on track to know what I need to do and feels great when I have done them. I may have some crazy individual days, but by the end of the week, they all get done.

That there's some good in this world,

Mr. Frodo....

and it's worth fighting for....

The Lord of the Rings

Bad Bob

You ever had that, "AHA" moment? The flash, when everything was suddenly clearer??? Your future, crystal clear, as you internalize the concept of "Weekly Goals" and how life changing that could be.

Maybe I was just at the right stage, to hear the same message, differently. Maybe the credit goes to those many seminar leaders that went before me, that said it differently to me, than I did, to me. Those pioneers of thought, that beat at the door of my brain, until it opened, just a crack..... and with that opening of the mind, "AHA...... I should be the coach."

That's it. If coach can get away with this "Weekly Goal" stuff, as an example of how to get paid for two minutes of work, I'm in. I thought of that long ago. One of my sales jobs, I had this boss that would ask how many calls we made or how many phone calls or blah, blah, blah.... at our meting, 4:30 every Friday afternoon.

That's when I first went with the weekly goals deal, besides, I always worked best under pressure. If I wait until the last minute, I am on fire and get a week's worth of calls made in a day. The more pressure, the better. One time, I was gonna get fired, if I didn't do something, I forget what. Man, I was great that morning, I was everywhere and got soooo much done. I never thought of sharing my secrets, with the other sales guys. Now I know, that I am a forward thinking, business genius. I used this whole "Weekly Shmeekly" thing, since my first job. .

Now that I have recognized my personal growth, I can not turn back. Yes, coach was a big part of getting me here, but that is the past. I must move on and find my own little grasshoppers. As I go forward, I shall be the coach. It is my duty to share what I know, with others, for a fee.

O.K., Little Grasshoppers...

Well, would you???

Chapter Twenty Three

My Mama Said

- If everyone jumped off a cliff, would you?
- Your face could freeze that way…
- Don't look a gift horse, in the mouth.
- That's a lazy man's load.
- Close the door. Were you born in a barn?
- Money doesn't grow on trees.
- Wear clean underwear, in case you get in an accident.
- Careful what you wish for.
- Yes, I am the boss of you.
- Because I'm your mother, that's why.
- I could have yelled for him.
- You'd lose your head, if it wasn't screwed on.
- I hope you have kids like you, someday.
- If I told you once, I told you a thousand times…
- I've got eyes in the back of my head, that's how.

You can be anything you want to be.

Thanks, mom. Love you.

Because it's not always easy to see,

where the danger may come from.

Script to talk to kids, about drugs/sex

We are salespeople. When we have a first appointment, with a huge prospect, we don't just go in and wing it. It is too important for that. We think about what we want to say and we practice.

The pros have a script, that they will follow. Their script, leads them through the process in a logical order, that they have pre-chosen, to assure the right outcome. Without the script, it is easy to jump ahead and miss a step. Sometimes, you can not come back to the beginning and the opportunity is gone. It is just too important, to not have a script.

The best of the best, anticipate objections and practice, how they will handle them. They seldom need to give, an off-the-cuff response, that they want a re-do on. Rather, they use premeditated words and pauses and inflections and facial expressions and...... and..... that they think, are the very best they could use, if that objection comes up. It is just too important to not practice.

Talking to our kids about sex or drugs or alcohol, is as important, as any appointment, that you, have ever had. We don't just bumble into a serious conversation by accident and wing it. We think about it ahead of time, and we practice. We choose the script, that we will use and think about what could go wrong. How will we handle it, if they......

I recommend a script that follows these steps.
Timing
Permission
Pause
Transition
The Problem
Question
Listen
Advice
Ending

Timing

We can not always decide when, we are going to have the conversation. It needs to be at the right time. Right time, for our child. Just because we choose to have the big talk after dinner, about 7:00, doesn't make it the right time. If when you go up to her bedroom, she is in the middle of some drama on the phone, with her teenaged friends, back out of the room. You need to catch her at a time, when she is not pre-occupied or stressed.

Permission

Before you begin, it is important to get their permission. It sets the right tone and lets them know, we need a few minutes. If they say no, respect that but do not tell them why you wanted to talk. Just save it, until the right time.
Try: Do you have a few minutes to talk about something?

Pause

I put pause here, but it is just the first, of many. When you get permission, do not just race into the conversation. Pause and sit and be reflective.

It lets them know that the topic is serious and assures they don't feel a "preaching" coming on. Throughout the entire conversation, it is important to pause and reflect often. It gives them time to speak more. They will feel less threatened and more likely to open up, if it goes slow. Pausing gives you a chance to not blow it, by over reacting.

Transition

I understand in today's world......
Or... It must be hard
Or... it's sure a lot harder for you than it was for me when I
    was your age.....
or... a personal story. If you can share a story about someone you know, that had a child that started the behavior you want to discuss, then tell them how bad it turned out. Let them know, that the kid's parents love him and are very sad.

The Problem

There are so many confusing messages about drugs (sex, alcohol) in todays culture.....
Or... I know drugs are everywhere at your school.....
Or... I know that you must see kids that are doing drugs...
Or... with all the movies and music, the whole sex thing
    must be confusing.....

The Question

Direct: Do you have any questions about all that?
Indirect: Does some of your age group, have a
problem with that?

Listen

If you can get your child to start to talk, shut up and listen. Do not jump in and solve things or give your parental opinion, at the first pause. Remember, pause, long and often. Ask them follow-up questions, to get them to explore the topic further.

Advice

Before you give advice, see if you can lead them into giving the advice. Try:
If you were the parent, how do you think…..
Or… do they talk about this at school and if so what do
they say?
Or… have you heard or read or Googled, any information
about this?
Or… give some statistics. Don't bore them but just give
one and tell her how scary that is. Ask their
thoughts about it.

Ending

The most important point of this topic, is to understand, this is not some big teaching moment. This is the beginning, of many more conversations to come. There is no end, to it. You are not solving anything today, but rather that the goal is to open a conversation, so comfortable, safe and assuring, that it will be easy for your child to re-visit the topic as it arises. The goal, is to make sure they feel safe and not judged, so that they feel like you are the one they can talk to, about a difficult and confusing topic.

Try: Poor kid, I'll give you a heads up, that I will bring this up once in awhile, because it's my job and I just love you too darn much not to. OK?

Or…   Keep me in the loop, will you

Or…   If any of your friends need help someday, know you
              can come talk to me.

Or…   I promise to be open with you and you know, I'll
              want to about talk stuff like this, again some
              time. Is that, alright?

          Handle anything they say, calmly. Be supportive and loving. Let them know that drugs are not allowed. It is not presented as, "No drugs if you're gonna live in my house" but rather "They just aren't acceptable to anybody that wants a good life. I want you to know that if ever you or a friend, needs help, there are ways to do that and I can help."

Bye, Felicia...

Bye Bob

Notes

Notes

Notes